STARMONT REFERENCE GUIDE NO. 3
ISSN O738-O127

The
Annotated
Guide to

STARTLING
STORIES

BORGO PRESS / WILDSIDE PRESS

www.wildsidepress.com

In fond memory of William F. Crawford and Manly Wade
Wellman, who helped fan the flame of fantasy for me in my
early years, even though they knew me not; and of Mike
Hodel, talk-show host par excellence, whom I sincerely
regret will never read this book or interview its author.

Library of Congress Cataloging-in-Publication Data

Gammell, Leon L.
    The annotated guide to Startling stories.

    (Starmont reference guide, ISSN 0738-0127 ; no. 3)
    1. Startling stories--Indexes.   2. Fantastic fic-
tion, American--Periodicals--Indexes.   3. Science fiction,
American--Periodicals--Indexes.   4. Science fiction--
Stories, plots, etc. 5. Fantastic fiction--Stories, plots,
etc. I. Startling stories. II. Title. III. Series.
PS648.F3G36   1986   813'.0876   86-6012
ISBN 0-930261-51-8
ISBN 0-930261-50-X (pbk.)

CONTENTS

Though only still in my middle forties, I am beginning to feel more and more like some fossilized relic of a far bygone era. Nowadays, if you mention the words "pulps" or "pulp mags," individuals in their twenties or younger are liable to regard you with utter lack of comprehension, wondering what kind of weird, old-fashioned jargon you old fogies are springing on them this time. Memories of the pulp era of American popular literature seem to be very rapidly passing out of ken of the general fund of public knowledge, except for diehard fanatic collectors and students of the genre like myself and a few others.

This is a shame, for the pulp era was a very rich and exciting period in our American literary history and deserves to be better remembered and understood by today's magazine readers, who have only a comparative handful of slicks and digests as a pitiful remnant to hint at what was once such a lush plethora of wonderfully variegated material. I will attempt to delineate some of the high points of the Golden Era of Pulp Magazine Writing, at least as far as the sub-genre of science fiction and fantasy is concerned, my own field of major personal interest, particularly those items which exerted most influence one way or another on the development of my career as a full-time science fiction fantasy fan, collector and amateur writer.

It was in the fifties when I first started reading pulp magazine science fiction. I was still in high school, and not yet possessed of sufficient funds to acquire those older issues which contained the kind of slam-bang space opera and thud-and-blunder headlong adventure that I then, and to a certain degree even today still do, enjoyed so immensely. Astounding Science Fiction was largely a bit too sophisticated for my admittedly adolescent and uncultivated tastes, and the once mighty Amazing Stories had been reduced by inept management and incompetent editorship to a level of juvenility and atrociously written drivel seldom equaled in any field of writing anywhere before or since. This left me with primarily two choices for my meager hoard of reading money, two magazines which lay squarely in the middle realm of competent literary craftsmanship and exciting writing that so widely separated the two afore-mentioned publications.

These were Thrilling Wonder Stories and its companion

1

magazine, my own personal favorite all-time science fiction periodical, the long-lamented and much-beloved <u>Startling Stories</u>. The latter was from the very first my favorite of the two, as every issue featured a full book-length novel rather than the short stories, novella and serials that were usually offered to the more or less discriminating fans in these pulps. There usually were a few short stories and novelettes of more or less interest to pad out each issue, but in those days I paid really very little attention to anything but the novel that was currently featured in the present issue. Except for the <u>Amazing</u> and <u>Wonder Quarterlies</u> of the late twenties and early thirties, I believe this was virtually a unique practice in the field of the science fiction pulp magazine, featuring a complete novel in each issue rather than the serialized installment novels that were run in the prestigious <u>Astounding Science Fiction</u> and elsewhere, and they certainly had a profound influence on my future development as a collector and fan, especially as most of them were of high imaginative content and usually more than ordinary literary competence. I would like to share with you some of my fond memories of the many grand novels that I read in the good old pages of <u>Startling Stories</u>, and try to acquaint latecomers to the science fiction field with the details of some largely overlooked and forgotten modern classics of the genre.

THE NOVELS

Weinbaum, Stanley G: THE BLACK FLAME (January, 1939)
I read this novel first in its (1900-1934) hardcover edition, issued by Fantasy Press in 1948, and did not acquire this premier issue of Startling Stories until I was out of school. Sequel to a novelette, "Dawn of Flame," later published in June of this same year in Thrilling Wonder Stories, this was a post-catastrophe-type novel, written by an acknowledged master of the science fiction genre and published posthumously several years after his un-timely death. Primarily a chronicle of the exploits of Mar-got, the Black Flame of Urbs, and her brother, Martin Sair, the Master, immortal rulers of a world ravaged and devas-tated by total war some centuries in the future, rising again to a high degree of technological civilization through the efforts of their special clique of immortal scientists and technicians, it also recounts the adventures of the revenant, Thomas Marshall Connor, kept in a state of suspended animation since the twentieth century by his electrical execution for murder till his resurrection by the scientists of the future, and how he finally wins as his bride the redoubtable Margot. Undoubtedly Weinbaum's greatest writing strength lay in his shorter works, the mar-velous novelettes depicting weird and alien forms of life on our sister planets of the Solar System, "A Martian Odyssey," "The Valley of Dreams," "Parasite Planet," "The Lotus Eaters," and others. But his novels tend to ramble and drag a bit, and The Black Flame is no exception. He also tended to irritatingly skim over potential points of inter-est in his rather thinly delineated future world of Urbs, introducing potentially fascinating characters like the mutant Metamorphs and Amphimorphs in one or two instances and then never using them again. However, with all its faults, this is far from the worst novel of its kind, and should be enjoyable reading for fans of the eighties as it was for those of the earlier decades, and the clear-cut figure of the strong-willed and ruthless Margot should find favor with today's women's rights advocates. Published with "Dawn of Flame" by Fantasy Press in 1948, and re-issued in paperback by Avon in the seventies.

Binder, Eando: THE IMPOSSIBLE WORLD (March, 1939)(1911-1974)
Good old fashioned, rip-roaring space opera with all

3

the stops out, and action foremost in the format. Invaders
from some trans-Plutonian planet without light intend to
conquer all the nine worlds of the Solar System and add them
to their mighty space empire. Doc Smith might have done
this sort of thing better, but Eando Binder's characters are
usually more human and believable. Anyway--rousing good
fun! As an aside, Eando Binder was a pseudonym for Otto O.
Binder, who wrote so many of the wonderfully imaginative and
often amusing stores for Captain Marvel Comics in the
forties and early fifties.

Hamilton, Edmond: THE PRISONER OF MARS (May,1939)(1904-1977)
        Interplanetary Prisoner of Zenda-type pastiche, by the
late grand old master of the space opera, largely forgotten
and neglected nowadays. Though born of an Earthly mother,
Philip Crain discovers that his father was the advance guard
of a Martian invasion force, accidentally marooned on Earth
for his entire lifetime, and his look-alike cousin is the
ruler of Mars. Accidentally transported to Mars via matter-
transmitter, he becomes quickly involved in the political
intrigue, swashbuckling action and eventual exchange of
identities that is the usual hallmark of this kind of story,
but Hamilton's novel is fast-paced and exciting, and should
make good reading even today, interspersed with interesting
characters to liven up the plot, among whom are a diabolical
mechanical brain manipulating the inhabitants of two worlds
for its own obscure purposes and a giant robot servant, almost human in its faithfulness and loyalty, perhaps a
foreshadowing of the irrepressible Grag of the Captain Future series. At the end of the story, Hamilton offers an
ingenious solution for resolving the difficulties of the two
warring planets, which stem largely from the Red World's
desperate need for water for her dead and desiccated oceans,
very simply accomplished by transporting the terrestrial
polar ice-caps to Mars through the matter-transmitters that
were to provide passage originally for her invading armies.
Who knows? Perhaps this will be the very method used in
terraforming Mars to make it livable for our first colonies
in the not-so-distant future, even as Hamilton's storybook
space-suits were the prototype for the ones used by today's
astronauts!

Wellman, Manly Wade: GIANTS FROM ETERNITY (July, 1939)
        A really different kind of   (1905-1986)
invasion-of-Earth story, by a fantasy giant active in the
field until his recent death. Earth is invaded by an over-
whelming flood of living red slime that devours everything
it touches, plants, animals, minerals, later evolving its

4

own peculiar kind of life-forms from its own, viscid substance. Mars and mighty Jupiter have been already overwhelmed and conquered by this ubiquitous substance, and
eventually Earth likewise will be totally absorbed by this
great red blob unless it can be stopped. Fortunately,
scientist Oliver Null Norfleet discovers that gas generated
from the red slime can be used to revitalize the dead, who
are then assured of a specious kind of immortality provided
they can keep in permanent contact with the invading
protozoan. With a fine touch of irony rather habitual with
Wellman, he uses it to resurrect deceased scientific
geniuses of the past, Giants from Eternity, to help fight
off the slimy red encroaching organism from outer space.
The story is well-written and fast-paced, as were most of
Startling's novels, good, bad or indifferent, and the revi-
talized historical figures—Sir Isaac Newton, Louis Pasteur,
Madame Curie, Charles Darwin, Edison—are rather well-drawn
and sympathetically portrayed, though just a little bit
over-sentimentalized perhaps. This was published in
hardcover in a more or less abridged edition in 1959 by
Avalon Press.

Williams, Robert Moore: THE BRIDGE TO EARTH (September,
1939)   (1907-1978)
        Run-of-the-mill invasion-of-earth story by an author
of average science fiction competence, but no giant in the
field by any stretch of the imagination. Williams was
author of the Zanthar novels published by Lancer in the
sixties, about which the less said the better. In this opus
intrepid John Dark foils the invasion of earth by the crafty
invaders of Marl, combined in treacherous alliance with the
European coalition, once before soundly trounced by the good
old boys of the American continent. The invaders' arch-spy,
Dunning, has since firmly entrenched himself in a position
of importance in the American government. There have been
worse novels on the subject than this one by far, but still
not one of the high points in the career of Startling
Stories.

Williamson, Jack: THE FORTRESS OF UTOPIA (November, 1939)
        Another goodie by a writer   (1908-   )
very active in the field today, still turning out masterpieces of the genre. In his early days, he was highly
touted as a second A. Merritt, no mean praise once, before
Merritt himself was largely forgotten and passed over, as he
is today. This one is very much in the vein of Thomas Cal-
vert McClary's Three Thousand Years, Rebirth, and similar
novels. A clique of scientists dedicated to saving the

5

Earth from disastrous collision with a rampaging comet some centuries in the future use a mind-erasing ray to hurl the world's inhabitants back into basic savagery, the better for them to evolve a super-civilization capable of saving the human race from the imminent catastrophe. In a fine touch of typical Williamson irony, it turns out to be the rebels against the Utopian civilization that arises after the universal mind-wash, rather than the Children of Utopia themselves, who provide the means of averting the approaching stellar cataclysm. This is a most engrossing novel on all levels, both thought-provoking and exciting escapist fare, and surely long overdue for the partial immortality of hardcovers, but for some reason seems to have been largely overlooked by Williamson devotees.

Hamilton, Edmond: THE THREE PLANETEERS (January, 1940)
    Typical rip-roaring Hamilton space opera. Nothing exceptional, but a rattling good yarn of three adventurers of the spaceways—an Earthling, a Martian and a Venusian—who join forces to combat the malevolent machinations of the evil League of the Cold Worlds to dominate the entire Solar System, including an heroic journey to the radioactive world of Erebus, outermost outpost of Sol's family. This was possibly the prototype novel for the later Captain Future novels that started in their own magazine, a companion to both Startling Stories and Thrilling Wonder Stories, in Spring of 1940.

Kuttner, Henry: WHEN NEW YORK VANISHED (March, 1940)
    Except for David Lindsay's   (1914-1958)
A Voyage to Arcturus, this is probably one of the most utterly fantastic novels I have ever had the pleasure to read, largely unknown to the modern fan public, penned by a science fiction genius cut off right in his prime by an untimely death from heart disease. This one has everything: adventure, comedy, mystery, all moving at a continual headlong pace that leaves the reader breathless. It winds up finally with New York City a model on a table in another dimension or parallel world's laboratory, a subject for the experiments of inconceivably monstrous beings attempting to save their alien civilization from being overwhelmed by hordes of highly specialized, insect-like creatures mutated by a strange new radioactive substance discovered far below the crust of their giant world. Words cannot really do this story justice, so if any of you are interested, I suggest you bogey on out and get hold of a copy of this magazine and read it, if you have to beg, borrow or even buy it.

6

Wellman, Manly Wade: TWICE IN TIME (May, 1940)
     Another classic by Mr. Wellman, this time combining
time travel with an engrossing historical novel of high adventure and intrigue during the period of the Italian
Renaissance. Leo Thrasher is catapulted by the Time Projec-
tor into one of the past ages of Europe, ultimately to discover that he is the famed and legendary scientist-artist of
Florence, Leonardo da Vinci. Perhaps a bit more fantasy
than real science fiction, but none the less still a great
yarn. Published in hardcover in 1957 by Avalon, which probably means a drastic abridgment. Read the original, if you
can, or the 1958 Galaxy Novel paperback edition.

Binder, Eando: FIVE STEPS TO TOMORROW (July, 1940)
     A science fiction version of Alexandre Dumas' Count of
Monte Cristo. In the year 2000, Richard Hale, President of
the Sub-Atlantic Tube Company, who plans to dig a tunnel
beneath the Atlantic Ocean between New York City and Le
Havre, France, thereby demonstrably lowering the high costs
of trans-ocean shipping and services, is framed on a
trumped-up charge and sent to the prison asteroid by the
Five, leaders of a world-wide crime syndicate whose profits
in legitimate enterprises would be seriously undercut by the
successful completion of his tunnel project. Eventually
Hale escapes from the prison asteroid by means of a trick
very much like the one used by Edmond Dantes to escape from
his prison. Now possessed of fabulous scientific secrets
learned from another prisoner, an aged scientist imprisoned
because he would not divulge his scientific marvels to those
in authority, he proceeds to mete out poetic justice to the
various members of the Five: glittering golden hands for
the man of greed, hands seemingly dripping with the blood of
guilt for a traitor, his best friend and his sweetheart's
father, a black, sooty skin for a man obsessed with physical
cleanliness, diminished stature for a military man of huge
and imposing physique, and partial transparency, allowing
the inner organs to show through the skin, for the literal
"Brain" of the world-wife conspiracy to control all
humanity. Nothing profound here, but a well-written story,
fast-paced and wonderfully imaginative. Published in paperback by Curtis in 1970.

Friend, Oscar J: THE KID FROM MARS (September, 1940)
     Llamkin, a totally naive and   (1897-1963)
unsophisticated young Martian, lands on Earth, searching for
an element rare on his planet to serve as catalyst for the
wholesale revitalization of Mars. Unfortunately, at first
everyone believes that it is all merely part of another

7

nutty publicity stunt to sell more films for Three Dimensional Pictures, and when they do finally believe, then, of course, everyone from the military to the underworld wants to exploit his considerable scientific knowledge for their purposes. There is a final space-flight back to Mars by Lambkin and some of his terrestrial friends, there to isolate the necessary catalytic element from material obtained on Earth, and a confrontation with Knaobians, green-skinned, bald-headed giants, one of the interior races of Mars, intent on sacrificing the terrestrials for the good of the Red Planet, before the Kid from Mars decides to take up permanent residence on Earth with his terrestrial sweetheart, masquerading as just another guy from Mars—Arizona. Light, entertaining, somewhat satirical as regards terrestrial happenings, but mainly an adventure story. One cannot help comparing this with today's Stranger In A Strange Land, by Robert A. Heinlein, on a similar but far more complicated and sophisticated theme. Published by Frederick Fell in hardcover in 1949, and by Kemsley in paperback in 1951.

Kuttner, Henry: A MILLION YEARS TO CONQUER (November, 1940)

Ardath, member of a star-roving civilization, highly advanced both technologically and emotionally, whose home world has been destroyed in a stellar catastrophe, is sole survivor when his interstellar colony-ship crashlands on an Earth still in the throes of dim, pre-Cambrian protohistory. Sealing himself in suspended animation in an atmosphere ship that he managed to salvage from the wreckage of the mother ship and place in an automatic orbit high above Earth, Ardath has his ultra sophisticated controls set to awaken him at regular intervals through the passing eons of terrestrial history, awaiting the evolution and development of a race with the requisite high level of intelligence and culture to be worthy of his civilization's legacy of tremendous scientific knowledge. Awakening at scattered intervals through the onrushing ages of earthly history, Ardath takes aboard his ship various specimens of humanity who have attained a higher than ordinary level of intelligence for their particular period of cultural development, to form the nucleus of a new super-race to which he will bequeath the massive learning of his vanished people sometime in the future—a villainous savage from Easter Island, an Atlantean priestess, a Roman gladiator, a Chinese philosopher. Eventually the variegated group of time-voyagers arrive in the twentieth century, only to find the world below afflicted by a strange and virulent plague that changes all those whom it does not kill outright into horrible glowing vampires that feed upon human vitality. With aid from a brilliant young

8

scientist of the twentieth century, and using his immense
fund of highly advanced technological and scientific
knowledge, Ardath devises a means of shielding Earth from
the pernicious effects of an energy cloud from outer space
that is causing the shining pestilence, despite violent
last-ditch opposition from the power-mad savage from Easter
Island. The climactic hand-to-hand battle-to-the-death between this brilliant but savagely brutal and twisted creature and the Roman gladiator is truly gripping. Perhaps a
rather crudely written novel in places, but a stupendous
plot! Highly imaginative, fast-paced reading. Vintage Kuttner at his best. Published by Popular Library in paperback
in 1968 as The Creature From Beyond Infinity.

Hamilton, Edmond: A YANK AT VALHALLA (January, 1941)
        Excellent mixture of lost race adventure and mythol-
ogy. Keith Masters discovers a hitherto unexplored region
at the North Pole where various prominent figures out of
Norse mythology--both the malevolent giants of Jotunheim and
the rugged AEsir gods of Asgard--are still alive and well,
kept in a state of perpetual immortality by radiations from
Muspelheim, the radioactive subterranean world directly
beneath their land, from whence all life on Earth originally
came. Much of the following plot concerns the escape of
Loki, the Norse god of evil, in this version a brilliant but
renegade AEsir scientist attempting to harness the forces of
nature in order to control first Asgard and then the world,
from the seemingly impregnable prison in which his fellow
Asgardians have trapped him with his two horrid pets, the
Fenris wolf and the Midgard serpent, terrifying monsters endowed with superior size and intelligence by their master's
scientific magic. Due to the machinations of his various
allies among the Jotuns, of course, Loki does ultimately escape from his scientifically-induced imprisonment, and from
then on the story's conclusion is well-nigh inevitable.
Ragnarok, Twilight of the Gods, comes, and the all-too-
mortal immortals of Asgard go down to their last defeat,
valiantly dragging their enemies with them into the darkness, while the subterranean world of Muspelheim disrupts
into final cataclysmic destruction beneath them. Published
in paperback first in 1950 as The Monsters of Jotunheim by
World Distributors/Sydney Pemberton, Manchester, and then in
1973, under its original title, by Ace as part of a double
novel.

Wellman, Manly Wade: SOJARR OF TITAN (March, 1941)
        One of my absolute favorites of the early Startling
novels, and one of Wellman's most exciting and richly im-

9

aginative early works. An interplanetary pastiche of Edgar
Rice Burrough's Tarzan novels, set on the giant moon of
Saturn, depicted as a wild, barbaric world, overgrown with
wilderness through which roam bands of mutually hostile
humans and humanoid aliens, traveling in wagon caravans like
other-worldly gypsies. Sojarr is a son of Earthly scientists and explorers who are the first potential colonists to
reach Titan but accidentally die in the attempt, leaving
their young child to grow up alone in the extraterrestrial
wilderness, menaced by predatory Titanian beasts and
unfriendly aliens. Eventually he is adopted by one of the
roaming bands of true humans, as opposed to the indigenous,
only vaguely manlike, inhabitants of Titan, who are their
inveterate and age-long foes. His terrific strength and
courage acquired and developed by his heroic sojourn in the
wilderness alone make him a most valuable asset to that
nomadic community. Not long after that, however, more
colonists from Earth arrive, a motley crew composed of
renegade scientists and fugitives from prison, seeking the
self-same goal as Sojarr's long-dead parents. Tension
mounts between the nomads and the colonists, especially when
a mysterious killer begins systematically decimating the
ranks of the latter, with the indigenous, exceedingly hostile Titanians uncompromisingly menacing to all the unwel-
come human interlopers. The story is finally resolved by
Sojarr's final unmasking of the mysterious and murderous
master villain, and the discovery of the human Titanians to
be terrestrial emigres, many times removed to be sure, from
sunken Atlantis, entitled to preeminent colony status under
the existing laws of Earth. A rip-roaring good novel in the
grand old pulp style, full of cliches and credulity-
straining coincidences perhaps, like so much of the old
pulpwriting but good fun throughout, and a landmark space-
adventure novel for Wellman. Published by Crestwood Publishing Co. in a rather severely abridged paperback, which
was where I first read it. Get the magazine version if you
can, for the full, uncut story.

Friend, Oscar J: THE WATER WORLD (May, 1941)
        Another of the post-catastrophe novels so common to
the pulp era of science fiction. This one contains some interesting descriptions of the drowned world of the future,
but unfortunately otherwise is not of particularly a high
level of overall imaginative content. It concerns a world
wherein all lands have been inundated by a second universal
Deluge, and humanity subsists precariously on artificial
island-platforms subject to the continual menace of wind and
storm and incursions by deep sea monsters of truly awe-

10

inspiring size and ferocity. Forced to flee their island home in a submarine of radical new design, the heroes of our story eventually discover a second group of survivors, living on the ocean bottom beneath a gigantic air-tight glass dome. These people have the living space and invulnerability to the elements so yearned after by the constantly cramped and harassed island dwellers, but they are gradually succumbing to a kind of wholesale racial degeneration due to lack of sunlight. The final chapters are involved with a horrendous battle with a race of plant men mutated from normal humans in the laboratory by the undersea dwellers in a desperate, last-ditch attempt to create a race capable of surviving without sunlight, but resulting instead in wholesale madness and paranoia. The novel ends on an optimistic note, as a resolution is formed to effect a partnership between the two groups of survivors whereby both island dwellers and bottom dwellers will be able to enjoy equally the benefits of their respective ways of life, differing but complementary.

Williamson, Jack: GATEWAY TO PARADISE (July, 1941)
     Another post-catastrophe novel, a bit better written than most, which is not surprising, seeing who is the author. In this one, Earth's moon, her seas and her atmosphere have been stolen by a rogue comet and whisked into the vastness of interstellar space, and life exists only beneath the colossal force-field that covers the entire United States of America, and in certain deeply-sunken, well-sealed mine shafts in the British Isles. The surviving Britishers, erroneously believing that the Yankees callously abandoned the rest of the world to die while taking refuge beneath their impregnable force-shield and embittered by their desperate daily struggle for a bare existence under horrendously hostile conditions, plot to puncture a hole in the shield, allowing Earth's last remnants of air to bleed out and dissipate over the pseudo-Lunar landscape. In the nick of time, however, Earth's moon returns to the Solar System, escaped from its temporary gravitational bondage to the rogue comet, bearing with it a goodly proportion of her parent world's air and water. Reaching Roch's Limit, Luna explodes and Earth's seas and atmosphere return to her in a rain of fiery meteors, harmless enough to America beneath her impregnable force-shield protection but totally devastating to the not nearly so well protected Brits in their mine-shelters. Thus, British Imperialism meets its ultimate just reward, and the American free enterprise system reigns supreme by default over all the terrestrial globe. Published in paperback in 1955 under the title Dome Around

11

America in an Ace Double Novel.

Burroughs, John Coleman and Hulbert: THE BOTTOM OF THE WORLD
September, 1941)   (1913-/1909-)
     The third and most ambitious collaboration by two of
the sons of Edgar Rice Burroughs, their two earlier works
being novelette-length interplanetaries, "The Man Without A
World" and "The Lightning Men," published in June, 1939, and
February, 1940, Thrilling Wonder Stories, respectively.
This novel concerns the invasion of the surface world by a
hitherto unknown race of highly pugnacious, amphibious
humanoids from beneath the sea, and features one highly interesting science fiction speculation throughout, never
before treated in a work of full novel-length as far as I am
aware, though the prestigious mainstream writer, F. Scott
Fitzgerald made it the subject of his Benjamin Button long
short story. For it seems that the invading amphibians are
subject to a totally different kind of life-style than any
experienced by their land-dwelling counterparts, being
hatched from egg-sacks in a condition of highly advanced
senility and growing steadily younger throughout the
remainder of their life-span, until they are finally and
literally unborn. In this truly epic extravaganza of
science fiction derring-do we have an archetypal mad scientist obsessed with the desire for eternal life who deserts
humanity's ranks in order to lead the submariners' invasion
of the lands of the surface world, a properly heroic and in-
domitable young scientist-hero, a properly beautiful and
demure heroine menaced at every turn by amorous villains and
monstrous monsters, villainous humanoids eager to subjugate
and enslave the air-breathing dwellers of the surface world;
in short, all the proper ingredients for a good old-
fashioned fantastic science fiction read of the ERB/Otis A.
Kline school with nearly all the stops pulled out and the
devil take the hindmost. It naturally invites comparison
with the work of their father, but I personally consider it
a competent enough job of writing, plotting, etc., to stand
on its own two--or four?-- feet as a minor classic of
science fiction adventure, developing and embellishing a
fantasy theme, that of the aging-in-reverse condition, that
was one of the few primary science fiction ideas apparently
overlooked by the practically all-encompassing imagination
of the elder Burroughs. Recommended as a period piece and
an early science fiction fantasy curiosity, if for no other
reason.

Millard, Joseph: THE GODS HATE KANSAS (November, 1941)
     Interesting variation of the   (1908-   )

invasion-of-earth theme, and sort of a precursor to novels like Heinlein's Puppet Masters, etc. A virulent new disease, the Scarlet Plague, breaks out in Kansas after the arrival of a strange new meteor, and people start dying off like flies. However, it soon develops that the casualties are not really dead, but merely in some sort of deep, catatonic state indistinguishable from death to Earthly science or medicine, and can then be utilized as host bodies by strange energy creatures from another world who accompanied the meteor to Kansas. Interestingly enough, these aliens are not invaders in the usual sense of the word, and not really inimical to the human race as such, intending to use Kansas as a temporary base of operations from which they may replenish their dwindling supply of host-bodies, as their original hosts, a sort of octopoid-creature from which they themselves once originally evolved, are steadily dying out. They also have a knotty philosophical problem, in that they perceive that their race is inevitably evolving toward a state of eventual union with the universal energy strata underlying the entire Cosmos, wherein they will lose their personal individuality, a concept they find most repugnant. Of course, the human hero of the story finds a solution to their problem in return for their leaving Kansas in peace, but I found it rather absurd that beings so highly evolved and advanced scientifically would not have thought of it themselves since it was so simple. However . . . ??? Reprinted in paperback in 1964 by Monarch. Some time in the seventies the British made a movie based on this story which was not half-bad as such things go, starring among others the distinguished English character actor, Michael Gough, as the leader of the aliens.

Wellman, Manly Wade: DEVIL'S PLANET (January, 1942)
     Another entry in Wellman's excellent future history series concerning the interaction of personal relationships between humans and the flower-headed natives of Mars. This one concerns breaking the stranglehold of ruthless earthly industrialists upon the vital water-resources of Mars, and is something of a murder mystery to boot, wherein the killer dispatches his victims with dummies stuffed with nitro. Reprinted in paperback in 1951 by World Distributors/Sidney Pemberton, Manchester.

Jameson, Malcolm: TARNISHED UTOPIA (March, 1942)(1891-1945)
     Written by the brother of the well-known radio actor, House Jameson (Henry Aldrich's father), while he was dying from cancer, this is another of those stories wherein the protagonist is sent into the future via the tried-and-true

13

suspended animation route, but a bit more interesting than most. Sort of a variant of the Buck Rogers theme. American Allen Winchester escapes from a Nazi prison camp and tunnels into a secret research laboratory where he unwittingly imbibes some experimental formula that casts him into a deep coma lasting centuries, from which he awakens to discover that the Orientals are undisputed masters of the Earth, having been victorious in World War II, and have colonized most of the Solar System as well. He eventually leads a successful revolt of the white slaves against their yellow overlords, capitalizing on his prowess as a botanist of no mean attainment in the doing. Easily the most interesting part of the novel is the description of the interplanetary zoological and botanical gardens established by the Orientals in the various craters of Luna, where young Winchester is put to work tending the exhibits of his new masters. Reprinted by Galaxy Novels in paperback in 1956.

Wells, Hal K: BLOOD ON THE SUN (May, 1942)
        From out of the distant past come creatures out of the folklore of every planet and race—the terrifying devil-beings of interplanetary myth and legend—to conquer the Solar System where once they ruled before, utilizing the hideous Brain Spider as their demoniac instrument of enslavement. Sounds corny and melodramatic, and it is. About average interplanetary pulp thriller.

Loomis, Noel: CITY OF GLASS (July, 1942)   (1905–1969)
        Interesting novel of a time very, very far in the future wherein humans of a drastically resource-depleted Earth are attempting to transmute themselves into a silicon-based form of life that can utilize the minerals and ores as food, and a spaceshipful of twentieth-centuryites transported thence by some kind of spacewarp mechanism attempt to reverse the process. Reprinted in 1956 as a Double-Action Paperback. It was also made into a B-grade science fiction movie in the fifties called World Without End, without the City of Glass but with the usual horrendous giant spiders and cyclopean human mutations, starring Hugh Marlowe, who really ought to have known better after his fine role in The Day The Earth Stood Still.

Morrison, William: TWO WORLDS TO SAVE (September, 1942)
pseudonym of Joseph Samachson   (1906-   )
        Probably one of the worst written and worst plotted novels ever to appear in the pages of Startling Stories, written at a time when most of the really good writers were out doing their bit for their country during World War II in

14

one capacity or another. There are some interesting descriptions of native life-forms on the Day- and Night-Sides of Mercury, but characterization is nil, overall plot structure and coherence is well-nigh nonexistent, and the villainous Mercurians seem as purposelessly inimical as old Doc Smith's Blackie DuQuesne.

Rocklynne, Ross: THE DAY OF THE CLOUD (November, 1942)
    Interesting world catastrophe   (1913-   ) novel by a well-known author still active today. Playboy engineer Harry Porter is catapulted into the far future to a time when the world faces imminent destruction by a deadly cosmic cloud and humanity is inexplicably suffering wide-scale brain deterioration. Better than average for this period.

Williams, Robert Moore: WORLD BEYOND THE SKY: (January, 1943)
    Mildly interesting story of wild adventures in a parallel dimensional "world beyond the sky" whose in-habitants, bronzed humanoids with pointed ears (shades of Mr. Spock!) are in danger of becoming enslaved by a paranoid dictator because their world has been a Utopian paradise for so very long that most of them have virtually forgotten the meaning of violence and war. A handful of intrepid earth-lings penetrate the erstwhile idyllic world of Sundra Unuum and attempt to aid a band of youthful rebels in their desperate fight for freedom, despite the existence of a traitor in their midst. Better written and plotted than many science fiction pulp novels of this period, but still nothing special. Good light reading for a couple hours' diversion.

Daniels, Norman A: SPEAK OF THE DEVIL (March, 1943)
    Mediocre story that is really more fantasy than science fiction, obviously a reject from Unknown or Weird Tales. Alex Craig, an actor portraying Satan on the stage somewhat unsuccessfully, has his brain waves temporarily iantensified by a scientist-friend's newest gadget, enabling him to establish contact with the real Devil himself, who offers him success on the stage in return for an unspecified length of time as one of his deputies on Earth. Due to the increased claim on his time and attention of really impor-tant matters resulting from World War II, Lucifer has few opportunities to attend to the sowing of minor brands of mischief on Earth and has pressing need of energetic and en-thusiastic deputies to do it for him. An interesting idea but one that has been done far more effectively both before

15

and since by far better writers than Daniels. According to
R. Reginald, this author wrote several of the Doc Savage
novels under the Street & Smith house pseudonym of Kenneth
Robeson, that was also used by the late Lester Dent, in my
opinion the far better writer of the two.

Cummings, Ray: WINGS OF ICARUS (June, 1943)   (1887-1957)
     The first and last novel by this grand old master of
the genre to appear in the pages of Startling Stories.
Regrettably this was not one of his better efforts. Barely
readable short novel of an expedition to Neptune to obtain
the necessary ingredients for the space fuel vital to the
continuance of human interplanetary civilization. Winged
humans, both friendly and inimical, and giant, many-headed
slugs are encountered along the way, as well as weird little
creatures that are practically nothing but walking eyeballs.

Rocklynne, Ross: PIRATES OF THE TIME TRAIL (Fall, 1943)
     Interesting variation of the old familiar time travel
theme. Warfare between different parallel time-worlds of
earthly history, where varying races and nationalities have
become dominant, English, French, Spanish, etc. Well written and fast paced, with good characterizations and a
catastrophic climax worthy of anything ever dreamed up by
ole Doc Smith. It is interesting that in this story, written during World War II, Rocklynne made his villains French
and English rather than Japanese, Germans and Italians. I'm
somewhat surprised it got past the censor because of morale
and propaganda purposes.

Jameson, Malcolm: THE GIANT ATOM (Winter, 1944)
     Excellent hard science fiction short novel by the
author of Tarnished Utopia. Defying the greedy tentacles of
General Atomics, Inc. that threaten to envelop all the in-
dustries of the world, scientist Steve Bennien struggles to
control a raging elemental force that he inadvertently
helped to unleash, a runaway reintegrating giant atom that
may eventually consume the entire planet. Reprinted a year
later in paperback by Bond-Charteris under the title Atomic
Bomb.

Daniels, Norman A: THE GREAT EGO (Spring, 1944)
     Another story that is much more fantasy than science
fiction, which reads like a reject from Unknown. Quite a
bit better than this author's earlier Speak of the Devil but
still far below par for the majority of material either from
Unknown or Startling Stories. Mild-mannered bank clerk Rod-
ney St. George is in reality a master sorcerer, combining

16

science and black magic in his attempts to enforce his ego upon the rest of mankind, turning into cats all persons who may in any way threaten his continued well-being.

Wellman, Manly Wade: STRANGERS ON THE HEIGHTS (Summer, 1944)
     Fascinating combination of science fiction and occultism by this talented and versatile author of such acknowledged classics of the genre as Giants From Eternity and Twice In Time, and creator of such unforgettable heroes as Judge Pursuivant, John Thunstone, and John the Ballad Singer. To avenge the death of a friend, Will Gardestang and Tommy Gatchell match wits--and fists--with a cult of Chilean devil-worshippers commanded by strange hairy beings that are natives of a totally alien plane of existence. There are Lovecraftian overtones galore as the Others, unfathomable, shape-changing devil-gods of primal myth and legend, attempt to manipulate and control the minds and souls of humanity for their own obscure purposes, combining science and alien magic to attain their cryptic ends. Reprinted in 1950 in paperback by World Distributors under the title, The Beasts From Beyond.

Brackett, Leigh: SHADOW OVER MARS (Fall, 1944)   (1915-1978)
     The first novel in Startling Stories by this highly talented and imaginative late wife of the late Edmond Hamilton, both of whom are sorely missed in the science fiction community today. Her novel, Sea Kings of Mars, published in Thrilling Wonder Stories some years later, is an acknowledged classic interplanetary, which exerted great influence on my early career as a fan and collector, and I was very well pleased to see that it had attained partial immortality and the sanctity of hard covers in a deluxe edition issued by Gregg Press under the title Sword of Rhiannon. Shadow Over Mars is not quite so imaginative as that one, and somewhat more down-to-earth for a science fiction novel, hardboiled and two-fisted almost as a Raymond Chandler or Dashiell Hammett detective story. It is well worth reading, though, concerning the efforts of adventurer Rick Urquhart to keep Mars from being totally dominated by the utterly ruthless owners of the Terran Exploitations Company. Hmm, anybody ever get the idea that science fiction writers don't like big business? Reprinted in 1951 in paperback by World Distributors/Sidney Pemberton, Manchester, and then again in 1961 as The Nemesis From Terra by Ace Double Novels.

Loomis, Noel: IRON MEN (Winter, 1945)
     Sequel to City of Glass, set at a much later date,

17

when mounting tensions between the Glassmen and the now numerous descendants of the inadvertent visitors from the twentieth century have reached a crisis, and a giant metal world supposedly equal in mass to about one third the composition of the entire Universe enters the Solar System, its weird metallic inhabitants offering to give the Earthlings a hand with their problems in return for assistance in solving their own peculiar difficulties. A very interesting satire, but I seriously question the logic and credibility of the existence of a world of such tremendous mass and density, unless it were somewhere near the center of the Universe and all other stellar bodies revolved around it.

Sterling, Brett: RED SUN OF DANGER (Spring, 1945)
    Even though Captain Future's own magazine had been dropped from publication, the character proved so popular that other novels were still written about him and appeared from time to time in the pages of Startling Stories. I understand this one was written by Edmond Hamilton, the originator of the series, under this house pseudonym for some unknown reason or other. This novel is typical of its kind, the usual fast-paced wild adventures among the inhabitants of various alien worlds, with a hint of mystery in this one, and even vaguely Lovecraftian overtones with the temporary revival in the final chapter of the Kangas, those mighty beings who once ruled the Universe before the rise of man or even man's immediate predecessors. Reprinted in 1968 in paperback by Popular Library as Danger Planet.

Long, Frank Belknap: THE HOLLOW WORLD (Summer, 1945)
    The culminating entry in this   (1903-   ) author's John Carstairs series, about a detective of the future who uses various kinds of animate plants to solve crimes and track down especially dangerous and resourceful felons. Unfortunately, Long never seemed to fully master the art of novel writing, and The Hollow World lacks the overall coherence and credibility of his shorter pieces. Moreover, the theme is hackneyed and poorly conceived, a mad genius plotting to overrun the entire Solar System with his hordes of sentient plant-men, striking from their secret lair in the interior of the hitherto undiscovered or undetected (except by him) tenth planet. Reprinted in hardcover in 1949 by Frederick Fell as part of John Carstairs, Space Detective.

Fearn, John Russell: AFTERMATH (Fall, 1945)   (1909-1960)
    Fast-paced novel by this highly versatile and fantastically prolific writer of the pulps who always borrowed

heavily from his own earlier ideas, probably best known today for his very imaginative Golden Amazon novels of the super-woman, Violet Ray, and his Liners of Time, wherein time-travel is established on a regular, full-time basis, like bus service or the Amtrak. This novel is especially interesting, as it is sort of a precursor to Paul Anderson's Brainwave, where a cosmic disaster raises the level of intelligence of every living organism on Earth, even to the lowliest amoeba and bacterium. However, Anderson's novel was mainly philosophical in tone, whereas Aftermath is strictly a wild and woolly thriller, like most of Fearn's work, ending in a world-wide cataclysm that virtually wipes out all unprotected life on the planet.

Hamilton, Edmond: OUTLAW WORLD (Winter, 1946)
    Edmond Hamilton's last Captain Future novel, though he wrote several excellent novelettes on the subject for Startling Stories a few years later. This one is a pretty fair entry in the series, concerning the Futuremen's search for the location of the secret outlaw world whose unscrupulous overlord is plotting a monumental crime coup with the aid of the radium he has been stealing all over the Solar System. Reprinted in 1969 in paperback by Popular Library.

Hammond, Keith: VALLEY OF THE FLAME (March, 1946) pseudonym of Henry Kuttner
    One of my absolute favorite science fiction pulp novels, with whose appearance I personally date the beginning of the Golden Age of Startling Stories. Written by the regrettably long-deceased Henry Kuttner under one of his many pseudonyms, it is a cracking good lost race yarn, telling of the hidden valley of Curipura and the strange people living there who were evolved from jaguars in thirty years. Mainly, however, it is the story of the fantastic Flame from a far universe with the power to control both time and matter, and of the various persons who sought to harness it for their own purposes--Brian Raft the adventurer, Parror the power-hungry, Craddock the hideously crippled delver after truth, Darum the mad king. It also tells of the horrible cavern of the Old Ones, that ancient race who once gained control of the Flame and then lost it, sinking thereafter into the lowest depths of bestial degeneracy, and the dread Garden of Kharn, whose strange master literally lived to eat! Reprinted in paperback by Ace in 1964.

Cross, Polton: OTHER EYES WATCHING (Spring, 1946) Pseudonym of John Russell Fearn
    Blinded in a tragic accident, Vera Brooks receives a

19

synthetic optics that unexpectedly enables her to see into the fourth dimension and view the evidence of a deserted alien civilization. Eventually she and her brother and Dr. Douglas Ashfield, who invented her artificial eyes, find a means of traveling physically thence to explore the alien megapolis whose original occupants seem to have departed elsewhere en masse without a trace. Other people are brought into the project and a colonization of the fourth dimensional world begun, but human greed and perversity eventually bring about a climactic confrontation with a higher power. This was also published in London in the same year in paperback as part of the Pendulum "Space-Time Series."

Kuttner, Henry: THE DARK WORLD (Summer, 1946)

Probably one of the first science fiction anti-hero stories. The main character, Ganelon, is a thoroughly unscrupulous individual with aspirations toward powers undreamed of by ordinary mortals. This novel has been called a rewrite of A. Merritt's Dwellers in the Mirage and with some justification, as the plots of the two novels are similar, but author Kuttner has endowed his story with more than enough originality and intrinsic interest for it to stand on its own feet. It is another of the excellent lost race yarns he wrote for Starling Stories during the forties, this one concerning the strange and terrible being, Llyr, whose chief servants are a vampire, a werewolf and a gorgon, and the courageous but unprincipled adventurer from the out-side world who dared to challenge their power. This was another variation on a theme that evidently interested Kuttner very much, judging from the number of times he used it, that of the super-man or exceptionally talented mutation born ahead of his time, and how such a being was inevitably warped and twisted into something quite alien and unsympathetic by pressure and conflict from the inferior and antagonistic normal humanity surrounding him. Recently, in an article for Fantasy Review, Marion Zimmer Bradley has asserted that C.L. Moore, Kuttner's wife with whom he collaborated on so many writing projects, has assured her that she wrote The Dark World in its entirety under her husband's name. This seems not unlikely when one considers that the style of this novel is consistent with the grim and downbeat tone of many of Moore's other works, notably the Northwest Smith IP tales, the Jirel of Joiry sword and sorcery stories, and the near-classic Gotterdamerung of the future, Judgment Night. Whoever wrote it, The Dark World is eminently readable and deserves to be much better known than it is. Reprinted by Ace paperbacks in 1965.

Wellman, Manly Wade: THE SOLAR INVASION (Fall, 1946)

The last Captain Future novel, written by an author other than Edmond Hamilton. This one concerns the return of the Futuremen's arch-enemy, Ul Quorn, the Magician of Mars, from his inadvertent exile in another dimension, leading an army of light-hating aliens from a world of darkness to overrun the Solar System. An interesting enough story in its own right and capably written as always by this fine author. Unfortunately, Mr. Wellman did not do his homework for this assignment and reread all the earlier novels in the series, with the result that he committed a monumental blunder in returning to life for this story President Carew of the System Government, who was murdered in Outlaws of the Moon by interplanetary gangsters and the Futuremen framed for the crime. Reprinted in 1966 by Popular Library in paperback.

Hamilton, Edmond: THE STAR OF LIFE (January, 1947)

Pretty fair interplanetary novel of the far future, somewhat more philosophical in tone than most of the works of this admittedly somewhat repetitive but still remarkably imaginative and entertaining author. This is the story of the Star of Life, a unique luminary whose rays endow humans with immortality and create profound mutations in their germ plasm, engendering entirely new species of humanity in their offspring--the Second Men, immortal and brilliant, who control interstellar civilization of the future, the Third Men, ruthless and paranoid, without any recognizable human trait except the insatiable desire for conquest, the Fourth Men, colossal intellects interested solely in scientific and philosophical experimentation and research. Full of cliches and overly convenient coincidences, but still a damned good read even today. Reprinted in hardcover in 1959 by Torquil, NY, and by Crest in paperback the same year.

Leinster, Murray: THE LAWS OF CHANCE (March, 1947)

Interesting novel by the premier   (1896-1975) dean of science fiction (real name, William Fitzgerald Jenkins), author of "The Mad Planet," "The Red Dust" and "Sidewise in Time," the master of depicting perfectly ordinary individuals caught up in circumstances quite outside previous human experience. This one is a post-catastrophe story with a new twist, telling ot the aftermath of a devastating atomic war and the one man who sought to harness the mathematical laws of chance for humanity's benefit. Reprinted in paperback in 1949? as Fight For Life by Crestwood Publishing Co. As an interesting aside, I found that Donald H. Tuck (Encyclopedia of Science Fiction and Fantasy, Volume I) has this novel down as being reprinted in Spring, 1954, in Fantastic Story Magazine, which had quite escaped my earlier notice.

Kuttner, Henry: LANDS OF THE EARTHQUAKE (May, 1947)

Still another excellent lost race novel by the fantastically prolific and indefatigable Mr. Kuttner, this one of a truly unusual nature. This is the only lost race story that I can think of that takes place in a world of a parallel dimension, except perhaps for Hannes Bok's Blue Flamingo, which was really more fantasy than science fiction, or P. Schuyler Miller's "Through the Vibrations" and "Cleon of Yzdral," which placed surviving Atlanteans and ancient Vikings in a world of a different vibratory wavelength. William Boyse, descendant of the Crusaders, finds that some of them are still alive in a strange parallel world, where time stands still and the landscape is in more or less constant motion, locked in a desperate struggle for survival with both mortal enemies and strange alien beings who can possess human bodies like a discarded suit of clothes.

Smith, George O: KINGDOM OF THE BLIND (July, 1947)

Minor novel by the author of   (1911-1981) such acknowledged science fiction classics as Venus Equilateral and Nomad. Scientists studying the mysterious Lawson Radiation from interstellar space inexplicably develop amnesia and subsequent decrease in intelligence for no apparent reason. It turns out to be due to the hypnotic influence of extraterrestrial aliens determined to keep the Earthlings from delving too deeply into certain secrets of the Universe. The big question is: are the aliens trying to keep mankind from penetrating secrets of the outer cosmos that are frankly too dangerous for them to handle at their present level of technological development, or are they scheming to prevent the terrestrials from gaining knowledge that might help stave off an imminent interstellar invasion? A revised version of this was published in hardcover by Gnome Press in 1959 as Path of Unreason.

Hammond, Keith: LORD OF THE STORM (September, 1947)

Minor novel by Henry Kuttner written under his Keith Hammond pseudonym, but still far above the average pulp science fiction for this period. Novel of the not-so-far future when weather control has become an accomplished fact, and the entire world is dominated by an aristocratic elite caste of scientists and bureaucrats. In this story Kuttner

22

introduces one of his most memorable villains, the devious and sinister La Boucherie, plotting to overturn civilization because he was shut out from the ruling elite as erratic and unfit.

Leinster, Murray: THE MAN IN THE IRON CAP (November, 1947)
    About average invasion-of-Earth novel with the familiar grisly little blood-drinking horrors dominating humanity by means of irresistible mental compulsion, all except for The Man In The Iron Cap, immune to their influence, who eventually devises a means to damp out their insidious mental dominance. Leinster was a master at portraying just plain people at grips with totally unfamiliar situations, and this novel is a fine example of his style. No classic perhaps, but certainly entertaining. Reprinted in 1954 by Ace Double Novels as The Brain Stealers.

Bok, Hannes: THE BLUE FLAMINGO (January, 1948) (1914-1964)
    One of the most unusual and imaginative lost race novels of the twentieth century, written by this sadly-neglected artist-author of great talent who dies so unnecessarily early in life. Regrettably, this pulp magazine version is cut from the original by at least half, and to read the full, unexpurgated version you must get the paperback reprint from Ballantine Books, issued as part of Lin Carter's Adult Fantasy Series in 1970 under the title, Beyond the Golden Stair. In either edition, however, it is a richly imaginative story of an utterly fantastic world existing in a series of interconnected parallel dimensions, with its entrance on Earth guarded by the fabulous Blue Flamingo who once was human. Another story that I just cannot do justice in words; you must read it for yourself for maximum effect. Enjoy.

Long, Wesley: ONE OF THREE (March, 1948) (Pseudonym of George O. Smith)
    Competent and readable alternate world novel, wherein three variant parallel time-worlds battle for personal survival; our own, Earth One, where the initial atom bomb test at Alamagordo was a complete success, Earth Two, where it unleashed a nuclear holocaust that nearly destroyed the planet and all life on it, and Earth Three, where it was a complete failure, resulting in widely diverging lines of scientific research.

Kuttner, Henry: THE MASK OF CIRCE (May, 1948)
    Still another of the fantastically prolific Mr. Kuttner's well-written and highly entertaining lost race

sagas. This one is even better than most, concerning a modern-day descendant of Jason who sailed with the Argonauts and searched for the fabled Golden Fleece, and how he discovered the ultimate, fantastic truth behind these myths. He finds the long-lost doorway to a secret world still living in the days and according to the ways of the old greek myths, dominated by grim Hecate, goddess of the darkness, and terrible, fiery Apollo, the smiling, ravening god of the sun. Reprinted in 1971 by Ace paperbacks.

Hamilton, Edmond: THE VALLEY OF CREATION (July, 1948)

Probably Edmond Hamilton's finest novel, at least in my personal estimation. Poetic, poignant, enthralling and exciting story of the hidden Valley of the Brotherhood, and how unscrupulous mercenaries from the outside world came there to use their modern weapons to turn the tide in an ancient war between men and beasts—eagles, wolves, tigers, horses—with human intellect and understanding. In a real whale of a cliffhanger climax, author Hamilton surpasses himself in explaining the ultimate origin of the Brotherhood and how and why men and the beasts are really and literally brothers. I really have some reservations on the genetic credibility of the idea he proposes in the chapter about the Cavern of Creation, but the writing is so fine and the story is so good as to overshadow anything as comparatively unimportant as scientific plausibility. Long overdue for hardcover respectability, if only in the Science Fiction Book Club cheapo format. Reprinted in 1964 in a somewhat revised edition by Lancer paperbacks.

Brown, Fredric: WHAT MAD UNIVERSE (September, 1948)

A real science fiction classic,   (1906-1972) undoubtedly the masterwork of this very fine author in this genre, often referred to as the O. Henry of science fiction because of his phenomenal facility at utilizing the short-short type of story. In this really incredible novel, however, he demonstrates his versatility and competence in any and all story lengths, telling of a parallel world of wildest fantasy, complete with intelligent, flying mechanical brains, nine-foot purple Bems from the Moon, cities dominated by night-roaming bands of anonymous killers after dark, and interstellar warfare with totally alien and unsympathetic creatures from Arcturus. This was one of the first science fiction novels I read after the material published by Wollheim and Avon, and it made a very profound impression on me, enough to leave me with a life-long predilection for parallel-world science fiction stories, the screwier and more imaginative the better. A life-long science fiction

24

fan of considerable critical astuteness and acumen has told me that he considers this novel to be Brown's own personal, loving tribute to the science fiction fans of his day, and this is certainly easy to believe, for the book reads like the chronicle of a fan-atic's ultimate dream-world completely out of control. Highly recommended to all fanactics—and normal humans! Reprinted in 1949 by E. P. Dutton in hardcover and by Bantam in paperback, also reprinted by Pennyfarthing Press in a deluxe, lavishly illustrated hardcover edition. Seriously recommended with all my heart to all fans and collectors of the science fiction genre.

Clarke, Arthur C: AGAINST THE FALL OF NIGHT (November, 1948)   (1917-   )
     Probably this well-known British author's most famous novel, the original nucleus and core of his masterpiece, The City and the Stars, concerning an Earth of the unthinkably distant future wherein the virtually immortal people of Diaspar and the folk of Lys, shorter-lived but incomparably more powerful mentally, share a nameless fear of the mighty Invaders from Outside, who may possibly one day come again, and of the two young boys who venture on a fantastic quest for answers to some of the age-old mysteries that have plagued terrestrial inhabitants since time immemorial. Reprinted in 1933 in hardcover by Gnome Press, then revised and expanded at least half again as much and retitled The City and the Stars, and issued in hardcover under that title in 1956 by Harcourt Brace and by Signet in paperback. It was also reprinted under the original title in 1954 by Permabook, and then by Pyramid in 1960, 1962 and 1967, as part of The Lion of Comarre and Against the Fall of Night, all in paperback.

Kuttner, Henry: THE TIME AXIS (January, 1949)
     Undoubtedly one of this author's most fantastic and imaginative tales, not a lost race novel this time but a story of the far distant future, wherein five involuntary time-travelers from the twentieth century merge with their alter ego/avatars of far future time to combat the universe-destroying menace of the Nekron and to attempt to save the totally fantastic City of Ea, mankind's ultimate triumph of technological creation, from cosmic corruption and decay. Reprinted in 1965 by Ace paperbacks.

Leinster, Murray: THE BLACK GALAXY (March, 1949)
     Probably the old master's most ambitious and imaginative novel for Starling Stories, concerning a totally ruthless race of interstellar marauders, who set monolith-like

25

traps on the moons and planets nearest to the worlds of technologically less advanced races so as to be forewarned when they are on the verge of space travel, appraising them that the time is ripe for them to move in with their space fleet and annihilate the indigenes with a weapon that consumes living tissue but leaves most artifacts intact for later looting and pillage. A certain knowledgeable science fiction fan whom I know from my apazine days sees in this a precursor of the Jovian sentinels in Arthur C. Clarke's 2001. Possible; but there are significant differences between the two. Clarke's Jovian monolith-makers appear to be largely benevolent in their ultimate objectives, while the builders of Leinster's lunar sentinel are wholly destructive and inimical to all other life-forms but their own. Clarke may have gotten the basic idea for the short story that was the prototype for his later novel and the film from reading Leinster's novel, but—who knows? Both were and are master story tellers in their own right, and it is always a moot point at best how much influence one author exerts upon another in this or any other genre. Anyway, to conclude. How a daring Earth scientist turns the tables on these cosmic creeps and eventually utilizes the gimmick of the Black Galaxy to accomplish their complete destruction is not so convincing or satisfying to me personally as when Doc Smith or John W. Campbell did the same thing, but it is still a fun read. Reprinted in paperback in 1954 by Galaxy Science Fiction Novels.

Harness, Charles L: FLIGHT INTO YESTERDAY (May, 1949)
    Intricately plotted and highly   (1915-   ) imaginative Van Vogtian-type time-travel paradox novel of the not-too-distant future, with enough plot twists and turns to keep even the most unappreciative reader guessing to the very last page. Basically, it is the story of the artificial superman, Alar, and his epic struggle to complete his mental and physical evolution that he may save mankind from destroying itself in a final suicidal war. But there are subplots galore and many fascinating characters occupy the reader's attention in case his interest in the main plot should momentarily lag, though none are so fascinating as the three ultimate villains, Haze-Gaunt, Shey and Thurmond. Here is surely a trio of the most horrendous nasties ever conceived by a science fiction writer prior to the creation of Darth Vader or Star Trek's Klingons; and wait till you learn the ultimate identity of the main villain's pet tarsier, who evidently traveled back in time with Alar the Thief. Unreservedly recommended. Reprinted in hardcover in 1953 by Avalon Books, New York, and then in 1955 under the

title, The Paradox Men, as an Ace Double Novel paperback. Under the new title, somewhat expanded from the original version, it was again reprinted in hardcover by Faber, London, in 1964. It was again reprinted under The Paradox Men title in hardcover by Crown Publishers, New York, in 1984.

Smith, George O: FIRE IN THE HEAVENS (July, 1949)
Very interesting hard-science science fiction novel by the author of Nomad and Venus Equilateral, about a flaw in the Law of the Conversation of Energy and what it has to do with periodically causing suns to go nova, including old Sol himself as in this story. Fascinating theory of sub-space energy and how tapping it could lead to practical interstellar space-flight to escape the solar instability. Reprinted by Avalon Books in hardcover and by Ace Double Novels in paperback in 1958.

Kuttner, Henry: THE PORTAL IN THE PICTURE (September, 1949)
Ironically humorous parallel world science fiction adventure story, of the type that Kuttner, writing in tandem with his equally talented wife, C. L. Moore, was to do so well later in his career, concerning a world in another dimension that could be reached only through a portal in a certain picture, and of the brash Earthman who journeyed there accidentally and of the strange culture he contacted therein dominated by an even stranger religion to which science was magic and magic was science. Retitled Beyond Earth's Gates and reprinted in 1954 by Ace Double Novels.

Leinster, Murray: THE OTHER WORLD (November, 1949)
Another competently written and highly readable science fiction adventure novel by the old master of such, this one with somewhat Charles Fortean overtones. Dick Blair accidentally discovers that the people of Earth are unwitting chattels of a powerful but decadent civilization inhabiting an adjoining dimension. He discovers how to outwit and even control the highly intelligent and savage wolf creatures that the other-worlders use as overseers and guards and begins his own personal rebellion against the secret tyranny of the decadents, who might possibly have themselves been descendants of Earth-people who millennia ago discovered the existence of the other dimensional world and the secret of traveling from one planet to the other. This was reprinted in 1954 by Dell paperbacks as part of Six Great Novels of Science Fiction, which also included Stuart Cloete's The Blast (atomic war aftermath), Robert Heinlein's Coventry (future history), James Blish's Surface Tension (interplanetary and biological engineering), Anthony

27

Boucher's <u>Barrier</u> (time travel), and Theodore Sturgeon's <u>Maturity</u> (high level homo superior story).

Van Vogt, A.E: THE SHADOW MEN (January, 1950) (1912-   )
     Van Vogt's only novel for <u>Startling Stories,</u> and definitely one of his minor efforts, but still quite entertaining and much less confusing in plot than many of his novels. It is a fairly typical Van Vogtian time-travel paradox novel, with the introduction of a rather novel agency called the Inter-Time Society For Psychological Adjustment, which purports to cure people's psychological hang-ups by having them murdered and then resurrected via time travel, among other equally bizarre ideas. There is also a fascinating picture of the future world of the mysterious Shadow Men, who control the Inter-Time Society, and the Planiacs and Tweeners, comparatively ordinary citizens, whom they dominate. Reprinted in 1953 as part of an Ace Double Novel, and then in 1967 as a single, both by Ace Paperbacks under the title <u>The Universe Maker.</u>

Daniels, Norman A: THE LADY IS A WITCH (March, 1950)
     By the author of <u>Speak of the Devil</u> and <u>The Great Ego,</u> another fantasy that would have been more at home in the pages of <u>Unknown</u> or <u>Weird Tales,</u> much better than either of his earlier efforts, and obviously written in imitation of Thorne Smith's posthumous novel, <u>The Passionate Witch,</u> that tells of the various strange antics of a witch in our modern world and which inspired among other things, the marvelous TV series of the sixties, <u>Bewitched,</u> starring Elizabeth Montgomery, Agnes Moorehead and Dick York.

MacDonald, John D: WINE OF THE DREAMERS (May, 1950)
     A real science fiction classic   (1916-   ) by an author really more noted for his mystery novels than anything else he has done, and the creator of a truly superb fantasy called <u>The Girl, The Gold Watch and Everything.</u> This story is a truly memorable one, telling of a decadent world of aliens whose space-spanning and mind-dominating entertainment machines enable them to continually cause havoc among the inhabitants of their three, long-forgotten colony worlds, one of which happens to be Earth. Reprinted in 1951 in hardcover by Greenberg: Publisher, New York, and in 1953, retitled <u>Planet of the Dreamers,</u> by Pocketbooks, Inc., in paperback.

Hamilton, Edmond: THE CITY AT WORLD'S END (July, 1950)
     A much more literate and adult novel than the old World Wrecker's earlier, cosmos-encompassing efforts,

detailing the somewhat startling adventures experienced by a small townful of twentieth century inhabitants suddenly catapulted unexpectedly by the detonation of the ultimate weapon into an incredibly remote future wherein old Sol is a virtually lifeless cinder and earth is a deserted and well-nigh forgotten world. This is a very well written and interesting novel indeed, though perhaps the sentimental aspects of it were a little overdone for my admittedly somewhat Philistine tastes, with many fascinating alien characters from the far-flung Galactic Confederation of allied worlds that now dominate the universe who come in reply to the stranded Earth-people's desperate distress call, particularly Gorr Holl, the man-bear mechanic from Capella. He's a corker. Reprinted in 1951 by Frederick Fell in hardcover, and then in paperback first in 1953 by Galaxy Science Fiction Novels, and then in 1954 by Corgi (England), and again in 1956 by Crest.

Jones, Raymond F: THE CYBERNETIC BRAINS (September, 1950)
    Truly a startling story,   (1915-   )
probably my favorite novel by this author, surpassing even his highly memorable Renaissance written for Astounding in the forties. This story concerns human brains that are kept alive after death and used to control machinery in various governmental laboratories in the not-so-distance future, and the successful attempts of two of those brains, a man and wife scientist team of considerable ability, to make themselves new artificial bodies with which to combat and defy the ruthless establishment that has heartlessly condemned them to this living hell. Mind-boggling story that really impressed me when I first read it in high school. Reprinted in hardcover by Avalon Books in 1962.

Vance, Jack: THE FIVE GOLD BANDS (November, 1950)(1916-   )
    The first novel by this highly literate and supremely sophisticated author that I ever read outside of his outstanding collection of interconnected novelettes about a far-distant future, The Dying Earth, and perhaps one of the first he ever wrote. Mild stuff compared to later mind-stunning epics of the genre such as Demon Princes series and his Planets of Adventure tetratology, but still quite entertaining and well-written. In this one interstellar adventurers Paddy Blackthorn and Fay Bursill attempt to learn the secret of the Five Gold Bands, thereby breaking the monopoly that five worlds of human-descended and mutated aliens have kept for centuries upon the production and dispersal of spaceships in the very remote future. Reprinted by Toby Press in 1953 in paperback under the title, The Space

<u>Pirate</u>, and then in 1963 by Ace Double Novels under the old title.

Gallun, Raymond Z: PASSPORT TO JUPITER (January, 1951)
     One of this author's very   (1910-   )
infrequent novels, and not too successful an effort as far
as I personally was concerned. Gallun is a master of the
short story and novelette form, turning out masterpieces
like "Old Faithful" and its sequels, "Seeds of the Dusk,"
"The Space Dwellers," etc. by the score, but the novel is a
different kettle of fish altogether, and he evidently never
quite got the hang of it, at least in this one. There are
some interesting moments in this interplanetary romance
which describes the events leading up to, during and after
the first human expedition to giant Jupiter, notably the
descriptions of the long-abandoned but still functioning
robot mechanisms of Ganymede, but these are few and far between, and the overall plot of the novel is a bit nebulous
and uncertain, with the general level of writing mostly
juvenile and uninspired. Disappointing performance from a
writer of his caliber.

Brackett, Leigh: THE STARMEN OF LLYRDIS (March, 1951)
     Excellent adult science fiction novel by the author-
wife of Edmond Hamilton, much more poetic and sentimental in
tone than her earlier, two-fisted, hard-boiled classic,
<u>Shadow Over Mars</u>. Basically it is the story of earthman
Michael Trehearne, and his adventures among the various inhabitants of the far-flung star-worlds when he learns that
he is actually a descendant of a starman from Llyrdis, the
world that completely monopolizes space-travel due to their
exclusive possession of the secret of genetically altering
human bodies to endure the terrific rigor and strain of
flight between the stars. Reprinted in hardcover in 1952 by
Gnome Press and by Museum Press, London, in 1954, both as
<u>The Starmen</u>, then in 1955 by Ace Double Novels as <u>The Galac-</u>
<u>tic Breed</u>, and then again in 1976 by Ballantine under the
original title.

Pratt, Fletcher: THE SEED FROM SPACE (May, 1951) (1897-1956)
     A very different kind of Earth-invasion story by one
of the most literate and knowledgeable writers in the genre,
the late collaborator with L. Sprague de Camp on many excellent works of fantasy written for John W. Campbell, Jr.'s
classic magazine of such, <u>Unknown</u> or <u>Unknown Worlds</u>, notably
<u>Land of Unreason</u> and <u>The Incomplete Enchanter</u>. This novel
is an engrossing psychological thriller and mystery, telling
of the gradual dominance during long ages of time of highly

30

intelligent plant-beings from another world that have as-
sumed the form of Earthly elm trees over the unsuspecting
minds of humanity by insidious telepathic control and
manipulation. Quite a bit above the usual invasion of Earth
from outer space theme for this period, as its author was
generally superior in writing ability to the average pulp
fiction writer.

West, Wallace: THE DARK TOWER (July, 1951)   (1900-1980)
        Good old-fashioned slam-bang space opera with all the
stops out, written by an author who had been around for a
few years, his first story, "The Last Man," having appeared
in a 1928 Amazing Stories. In this one descendants of
colonists from an Earth destroyed by a catastrophic atomic
war who migrated to Centaurus constellation have to battle
for survival against both their own barbarian cousins who
settled in the Proxima Cluster, led by warlord Rolph and his
wildcat sister, and the mysterious and ancient Siriuns, who
wield frightening telepathic powers through the medium of
the Dark Tower, some kind of tremendously potent mechanical
mind power enhancer. Reprinted by Avalon Books in hardcover
in 1961, then in paperback in Airmont the next year, both
times as The Memory Bank.

Merwin, Jr., Sam: HOUSE OF MANY WORLDS (September, 1951)
        Interesting story about travel   (1910-   )
between various alternate time-worlds of parallel history,
and of the secret organization that regulated and controlled
that traffic. One of the first science fiction stories that
I know of to feature a black hero among its other major
characters, using a contemporary setting rather than an historical one, like Haggard's novels of the Zulus of
nineteenth century Africa. In this case we have a modern-
ized version of the redoubtable John Henry, the pile-driving
champion of American popular folklore. Reprinted (enlarged)
in hardcover by Doubleday in 1951, and then the next year in
paperback by Galaxy Science Fiction Novels.

Russell, Eric Frank: THE STAR WATCHERS (November, 1951)
        The first science fiction novel   (1905-1978)
written for Startling Stories by this very talented British
author. Another of his excellent "we are property"-type
novels, like Sinister Barrier that he wrote for Unknown and
Dreadful Sanctuary for Astounding, only written on a much
more lavish scale than either of those earlier works. In
this novel mankind's secret guardians must keep hidden even
from their own people the secret of their ultimate destiny
lest knowledge of it somehow leak out to the powerful and

31

aggressive Denebs who control most of the material Universe, and at the same time quell a suicidal war that has broken out between the normal homo sapiens of the Solar System and the many species of variously talented mutants that have developed by gene contamination from cosmic radiation encountered during space flight. Written in the same wryly humorous style that he utilized so effectively in Dreadful Sanctuary. Retitled Sentinels From Space and reprinted by Ace Double Novels in 1953, and by Avalon Books, New York, in hardcover.

Leinster, Murray: JOURNEY TO BARKUT (January, 1952)
This is quite a departure from this writer's usual type of story, as he usually stayed pretty much with comparatively--down to Earth!--straight science fiction, like his Man In the Iron Car, Black Galaxy, and Lands of Chance. This story shows that he was well able to write pure fantasy, though, whenever he chose to, and I wish he had more often. This novel concerns the incredible adventures of an average American male of the twentieth century who somehow finds entry to a parallel time world where creatures straight out of the Arabian Nights--djinn and efreets, beings like animated atomic bombs that can alter their bodily shape at will--are the dominant form of life, and mankind is a comparatively inferior species. Written in the style of the old Unknown, particularly that of L. Ren Hubbard, who wrote wonderful fantasies before he turned his attentions primarily to making several fortunes out of his Dianetics drivel. This was reprinted in 1954 by Ace Double Novels as Gateway To Elsewhere, which I discovered from Tuck's Encyclopedia of Science Fiction and Fantasy was the title under which it originally appeared in 1950, or the first installment of it, in Fantasy Book #7, which publication evidently folded before the serial could be completed.

St. Clair, Margaret: VULCAN'S DOLLS (February, 1952)
The first novel for   (1911-   )
Startling Stories by this very talented female author, who evidently was another of those writers who functioned best in the shorter form of writing and never quite got the hang of doing the novel properly, as this story is a little disjointed in spots but the plot is interesting enough and the characterization adequate to carry it through. It is primarily the story of the mysterious architect-god, Vulcan, and his struggle with his rebellious pupil, Mulciber, for the control of human destiny and to allow free and uninhibited reign to the spread of future human mutations, and of Vulcan's wondrous dolls, who seemed veritably human.

32

Reprinted in 1956 by Ace Double Novels as <u>Agent of the Unknown</u>.

Kuttner, Henry: THE WELL OF THE WORLDS (March, 1952)
One of this fantastically prolific and talented author's final and most successful novels, probably his best for <u>Startling Stories</u>. This is an incredibly imaginative story of the inhabitants of an alternate world, who live on a congeries of continually floating islands instead of on planets like we prosaic terrestrials, drifting between the Overworld and the Underworld, both of which harbor biologically superior but diverse and mutually antagonistic species, whose ultimate secret forms the crux of the whole plot and the punch line to the last pages of the novel. Well-written and fast-paced, like most of his work, a culminating masterpiece for his myriad and diverse efforts for <u>Startling Stories</u>, which began with the free-wheeling and utterly bizarre <u>When New York Vanished</u> back in 1940. Reprinted by Ace paperback in 1965 and by Galaxy Science Fiction Novels in 1953.

DeCamp, L. Sprague: THE GLORY THAT WAS (April, 1952)
The first novel for <u>Startling</u> (1907-)
<u>Stories</u> by this most erudite and opinionated writer, who has tried his hand at everything from Conan pastiches, historical novels like <u>The Bronze God of Rhodes</u> and <u>An Elephant for Aristotle</u>, non-fiction works like <u>Lost Continents</u> and <u>Spirits, Stars and Spells</u>, biographies of other writers like his masterful one on Lovecraft, or straight science fiction like <u>Divide and Rule</u> and <u>The Stolen Dormouse</u> to whimsical fantasies like <u>The Undesired Princess</u> and <u>Solomon's Stone</u>. In this very interesting story he tells of a madman's recreation of a bit of Classical Greece in the world of the twenty-seventh century, and of two modern men who stumbled upon this seemingly lost world, experiencing a kind of time travel without actually physically traveling backward in time. Definitely for those science fiction fans who like something a bit out of the ordinary. Reprinted in hardcover by Avalon Books in 1960.

Smith, George O: THE HELLFLOWER (May, 1952)
By the versatile author of many excellent hard-science science fiction novels, such as <u>Pattern For Conquest</u> and <u>Fire In the Heavens</u>, a very interesting story that is a sort of science fiction version of a hard-boiled mystery-adventure novel, concerning the attempt of a cashiered space pilot to infiltrate the insidious hellflower dope ring, a far-flung criminal organization with tentacles reaching into

every inhabited planet in the Solar System, spreading a particularly hideous addiction that completely enslaves human women, body and soul. Reprinted in hardcover in 1953 by Abelard Press, then by Bodley Head, London, in 1955, and finally in 1957 by Pyramid paperbacks.

Williamson, Jack: DRAGON'S ISLAND (June, 1952)
    This novel represents quite a radical change in policy from Startling Stories' usual one, as it is an abridged reprint of an earlier 1951 hardcover edition published by Simon & Schuster. It is a highly interesting story of how artificial mutations were induced in certain specimens of homo sapiens by genetic engineering and an entirely new species of humanity created—homo excellens, or, as their enemies referred to them, the not-men, possessed of seemingly superhuman powers and abilities. It reminds me of A.E. van Vogt's Slan in a way, with mystery and intrigue abounding in every page, as homo sapiens and the not-men battle each other desperately for survival both in the open and undercover, until at long last the ultimate secret of the dragon's island is revealed to both.

Crossen, Kendell Foster: PASSPORT TO PAX (July, 1952)
    Novel of thirty-first century   (1910-1982) interstellar big business ethics (or lack of them) by a leading science fiction humorist, whose earlier novella, Restricted Clientele, delightfully parodied and burlesqued human affairs and economic values in a fashion that Voltaire himself would undoubtedly have found irresistibly ridiculous. This novel is rather more serious in tone than most of his work that I have encountered and is mainly a story of inter-Galactic sabotage and espionage, as the planets of Regulus, Nike and Pax, wage no-holds-barred economic warfare against the equally ruthless big business cartel of the A.G.I. There are a few surprises at the end, though, that you may not be expecting; I know I certainly wasn't.

Farmer, Philip Jose: THE LOVERS (August, 1952) (1918-   )
    The first science fiction novel by a supremely talented and versatile author who has since become a legend in his own time. Though pretty mild stuff by today's standards, this was considered quite a precedent-breaking novel in 1952, shattering all the unwritten laws enforcing the sexual taboos then pretty much universally prevalent throughout science fiction literature. Basically, this is the story of the love of an Earthman for a female inhabitant of a planet in a far distant star system, who eventually

turns out to be a sort of giant insect of a type that mimics the female of the human species in order to have sexual intercourse with the male, even though pregnancy to these alien females means inevitable death of a particularly gruesome variety. Aside from all ·this, it is a fascinating word-picture of a world radically different from our own, and of the many and diverse strange forms of alien life inhabiting it. Reprinted by Ballantine Books first in 1961 in paperback, and then by Ballantine Books/Del Rey in hardcover in 1979.

Vance, Jack: BIG PLANET (September, 1952)
    An excellent science fiction adventure novel by one of the most sophisticated masters of the English language writing in the genre today, whom I personally would term the Henry James of science fiction. This is possibly his finest work to date. It is a wild and woolly saga of a band of stranded Earthmen and their odyssey over the strange terrain of a giant planet in another star-system that is inhabited by numerous bizarre cultures exiled from Mother Earth because their laws and customs proved incompatible with the view of the majority of her inhabitants. Imaginative, fast-paced, well written, with plenty of Vance's wry wit to further enliven and invigorate the plot and dialogue. Reprinted by Avalon, New York, in hardcover, and by Ace Double Novels in paperback, both in 1957, and then again in 1978 in a deluxe, lavishly illustrated edition by Underwood & Miller.

Elliott, Bruce: ASYLUM EARTH (October, 1952)   (1915-1973)
    Unusual novel that is a very interesting mixture of magic, folklore and science fiction that would have certainly gone over well in the hallowed pages of the good old Unknown, published by Street & Smith from 1939-1943. This is a Charles Fortean-type story, of the always interesting, intellectually stimulating, we-are-property variety, with a few new twists, such as giving an explanation for the widespread prevalence of serious mental disorders among the inhabitants of Earth, rather different from the one postulated by Eric Frank Russell in Dreadful Sanctuary but with some similarities in plot and idea. I read another story by Mr. Elliott years ago, a short called "Wolves Don't Cry," sort of a werewolf yarn in reverse, wherein a real wolf gets inadvertently changed into a human being and has to find a way to change back again, which impressed me very much. I recently discovered that Mr. Elliott has been deceased for some years now, much to my regret, and I certainly wish he had written much more fantasy than he did, or somebody would

enlighten me where it can be found if I have been missing it, because I like his style very much. Reprinted by Belmont paperbacks in 1968.

Dee, Roger: THE STAR DICE (November, 1952) Pseudonym of Roger D. Aycock   (1914-   )
First science fiction novel by a writer hitherto known only for his shorter works ("Paradox Planet," "The Obligation"), and very good for a first try, too. In this story, Paul Shannon, spaceman-engineer for Solar Services, returns to Earth after being marooned on Io, moon of Jupiter, for two years, only to find his native world caught tight in the grip of the benevolent domination of the Cubes, strange creatures from outer space able to endow their human contacts with mental serenity and inner peace-of-mind but at the expense of all those aggressive, high-survival-factor instincts that have largely contributed to maintaining mankind's dominant position on this planet. The stranded Earthman returning to a profoundly changed world was a plot that had whiskers on it even back in the thirties, but a good writer can breathe new life into even the hoariest ideas, and Mr. Dee saves this one with the strength of his writing and the freshness of his approach. Reprinted in 1954 by Ace Double Novels as An Earth Gone Mad.

Pratt, Fletcher: THE LONG VIEW (December, 1952)
Brilliant short novel of far-future interstellar politics, much of which takes place on Uller, a fascinating world based upon a silicon life-basis rather than the usual carbon-and-oxygen one, painstakingly detailed and plotted by this highly erudite and scholarly writer, whose untimely demise in 1956 was sincerely mourned in all quarters of the science fiction community. This story evidently first appeared in a hardcover anthology issued in this same year by Twayne, New York, The Petrified Planet, edited by Pratt. It contains three short novels, independent of one another, but using as a common background the silicon-life world of Uller, devised by Dr. J. D. Clark. The other two entries were Uller Uprising, by H. Beam Piper, and Daughters of Earth, by Judith Merrill; the first of which has just recently been reprinted by Ace paperbacks.

Knight, Damon: DOUBLE MEANING (January, 1953)   (1922-   )
The first novel for Startling Stories by this acerbic science fiction critic and talented writer, author of In Search of Wonder and Hell's Pavement. While I do not personally agree with most of Mr. Knight's views of many of the classic authors of science fiction and fantasy, such as A.

Merritt, H. P. Lovecraft, A.E. van Vogt and Robert E. Howard, to name only a few, I find his critical reviews and articles most stimulating reading, besides being extremely entertaining and oftentimes quite amusing. I have never been as fond of his works of fiction as I have of his critiques, usually preferring his short stories and novelettes to his novels, but this one seems of rather more than casual interest, telling of the desperate struggle of a particularly obnoxious totalitarian Earth-dominated interstellar empire of the twenty-sixth century with the wholly alien Rithians and the supposedly backward peoples of the despised colonial Outworlds. Reprinted in paperback by Ace Double Novels in 1964 as The Rithian Terror.

Smith, George O: TROUBLED STAR (February, 1953)
    Mildly amusing and slightly satirical space opera by the author of The Hellflower and Nomad. In this one Dusty Britton, phony movie idol star of a long series of Space Patrol epics, is mistaken by visitors from the capitol of Galactic Civilization, Marandis, for an actual high official in the non-existent terrestrial Space Patrol and given the unenviable task of preparing humanity for a change of suns, as the Marandanians intend to turn old Sol into an interstellar beacon for a projected space highway that would render Earth uninhabitable for humans unless it were moved bodily by the alien science to orbit around a new star. Reprinted in 1957 in hardcover by Avalon, New York, and then in 1959 in paperback by Beacon Galaxy Novels.

Merwin, Jr., Sam: CENTAURUS (March,1953)
    Very interesting blend of time travel and interplanetary adventure, with a bit of the hardboiled detective school and flying saucers menacing a bewildered and bemused terrestrial population thrown in for good measure. A citizen of ancient Rome is inadvertently snatched ahead into the twentieth century to become the protege of a world-famous scientist--and the lover of his wife--, with an involuntary stopover on the way at a planet of Centaurus as guests of the wholly alien saucer people who later trail him all the way to Earth to exact retribution for the accidental killing of some of their leading citizens.

Crossen, Kendell Foster: HALOS, INC. (April, 1953)
    Another of this author's highly amusing satires on big business and human morals and customs, set in the thirty-first century, when mankind has spread to the stars and taken their advertising techniques and sometimes dubious salesmanship methods to sucker and con other worlds and

37

other races than their own. This is a sequel to his
novella, "Things of Distinction," in the March 1952 Startling Stories, wherein Jerry Ransom tried to sell hats to intelligent lightning bugs with natural halos until he hit
upon the bright (!) idea of going into partnership with some
of his erstwhile insectile clients and selling their
luminous products to humans instead as a brilliant new in-
novation in clothing styles. In this novel the unscrupulous
Dibble clan return to further plague the harassed young
business executive, who was formerly their long-suffering
employee in the earlier story, as heads of a fantastic new
religion that bids fair to take over virtually all of human
interstellar civilization--and big business--by a shrewd and
bloodless coup.

Pratt, Fletcher: THE CONDITIONED CAPTAIN (May, 1953)
    Highly interesting and imaginative novel of intrigue,
politics and James Bond-style espionage in the far future,
with an interplanetary setting somewhat loosely based upon
the epic Greek myth of the voyage of the Argonauts in search
of the fabled Golden Fleece, with a planet dominated by
women who have overturned the rule of their erstwhile mas-
culine masters (Lemnos), and an Irish-colonized world called
Danaan whose people have developed a radical new kind of
neptunium motor for spaceships that the rest of space-faring
humanity needs desperately (Colchis), besides a pair of
highly telepathic twin stowaways and a Russian general of
ground troops anxious, like Hercules of old, to find more
labors to perform. Good fun. Published by Ballantine Books
under the title, The Undying Fire, in 1953, both in
hardcover and in paperback.

Farmer, Philip Jose: MOTH AND RUST (June, 1953)
    The sequel to this writer's iconoclastic masterpiece,
The Lovers (Startling Stories, July, 1952) in which he
brings the human-mimicking giant insects of Ozagen of the
earlier novel to Earth itself, at a time when the world is
embroiled in a frantic phantasmagoria of class-wars, racial
struggles, and utterly nonsensical theological disputes (are
there any other kind?) and the dominant religion seems to be
the worship of Isaac Sigmen, the semi-divine Forerunner,
some kind of extraordinary temporal time traveler who is
momentarily expected to appear and proclaim the Day of
Timestop, when all his faithful will be rewarded and his
enemies, the followers of Jude Changer, his half-brother,
the diabolical Backrunner, summarily punished. Fascinating
if somewhat confusing novel, and probably one of the longest
Startling Stories ever published. Reprinted in paperback by

Galaxy & Beacon Books in 1960 as A Woman A Day, and then by
Lancer in 1968 as The Day of Timestop and in 1970 as Timestop.

Merwin, Jr., Sam: JOURNEY TO MISENUM (August, 1953)
      Sequel to this writer/editor's earlier House of Many
Worlds in the same magazine. Entertaining account of Time
Watcher Elspeth Marriner's desperate attempts to avoid a
technological overlap between three widely divergent time-
tracks of terrestrial history, our modern Atomic Age world,
Rome of two thousand years past, and Heartland, so poisoned
by deadly radioactivity that most of its world is unin-
habitable, ruled by a ruthless and despotic matriarchy who
believe that a man's proper place is under a woman's thumb.
Reprinted by Ace Double Novels as Three Faces of Time in
1956.

Merwin, Jr., Sam: THE WHITE WIDOWS (October, 1953)
      Something of a first for Startling Stories, as this is
the first time I can recall that the same author had a novel
featured in two consecutive issues, even in the most
prolific heydays of Edmond Hamilton and Henry Kuttner,
though undoubtedly the fact that Sam Merwin, Jr. was
formerly the editor of Startling Stories probably had something to do with it. This is one of those war-of-the-sexes
novels, telling of the discovery of a centuries-old conspiracy of Amazon females to dominate humanity by spreading
hemophilia and other male-weakening diseases throughout the
world, and how Larry Finlay and Mayne Cornaman attempted to
prove their existence and expose their machinations to
universal scrutiny. Reprinted in hardcover in 1953 by
Doubleday, and then in paperback in 1960 by Galaxy Novels
and Beacon Books under the title, The Sex War.

Tucker, Wilson: THE TIME MASTERS (January, 1954) (1914-   )
      Very interesting combination of immortal man story and
interplanetary, with plenty of intrigue and mystery tossed
in for good measure. Extremely long-lived interstellar
travelers are stranded on Earth when their spaceship is
wrecked, and manage to survive among the natives from the
earliest beginnings of civilization till the present day.
The hero of the tale gave rise to the Gilgamesh legend of
old Sumeria, among other things, by his search for the
waters of youth, or modern heavy-water, to use the correct
scientific parlance, to continue his seemingly immortal
life. Between him and another survivor of the wrecked
spaceship's crew, a female of singularly lax morals and
ruthless determination, there exists a bitter feud of long-

standing, reaching from the dim past of pre-history clear
into the Atomic Age of the twentieth century. Reprinted in
paperback by Signet in 1953, July, which was where I first
read it, but according to Reginald's Science Fiction and
Fantasy Literature it first appeared in a hardcover edition
in 1953 published by Rinehart & Co., New York, so this
magazine appearance must have been another reprint, like
Jack Williamson's Dragon's Island in the June, 1952 issue.

Vance, Jack: THE HOUSES OF ISZM (Spring, 1954)
     By the author of Dragon Masters and Big Planet,
another excellent story of interstellar intrigue and adventure in the far future. In this short novel, the planet
Iszm holds a monopoly on supplying the other worlds of the
galaxy with houses that are actually living, growing plants,
grown and adapted to fit the needs of their owners by the
master Iszic botanists, and Farr Sainh must somehow steal a
female house-seed and sneak it off the planet to break this
highly lucrative monopoly of living quarters. As usual with
Vance's work, well-written, sophisticated and wryly humorous
in spots, with just a touch of gruesomeness in places and at
times when you would least expect it. Reprinted in paperback by Ace Double Novels in 1964, and then in 1983 by Un-
derwood & Miller in one of their very lavish, deluxe, illustrated, hardcover editions.

Pratt, Fletcher: THE SPIRAL OF THE AGES (Summer, 1954)
     Rather interesting time-travel novel by the author of
The Seed From Space and The Long View, somewhat better written and more thoroughly researched and thought-out than most
stories of this type. Using his scientist friend's new
time-traveling device, the tempolator, Robert Anthony sends
his mind back to the body of an early chronicler in Celtic
Britain to foil Mordred's conspiracy against King Arthur.
He returns to his own time to find the world radically
changed from the way he knew it as a result of his unwise
tampering with history. An attempt to correct this makes a
subsequent journey into the time-stream obligatory to yet
another period of long-dead history. A very scholarly and
well-written piece of work, but fast-paced and full of adventure and derring-do as well.

Smith, George O: SPACEMEN LOST (Fall, 1954)
     Smith's last novel for Startling Stories, but one of
his best. Engrossing story of an interstellar space-search
by terrestrial spacemen for a wrecked space-liner's
lifeships and their survivors while hostile humanoids from a
powerful and alien civilization observe their methods and

plan the best way to move in and subjugate Earth and her colonies. Excellent hard science fiction story by a long-time master of such material. Reprinted in hardcover by Avalon Books in 1959, and in paperback the following year by Ace Double Novels, both under the title, Lost In Space.

Anderson, Poul: THE SNOWS OF GANYMEDE (Winter, 1955)
        The first and last novel for   (1926-   )
Startling Stories by this very popular modern science fiction writer, whom I regard as rather a latter-day E. E.
Smith, only a much more literate and coherent artist. This
novel is part of his first future history series, now dis-
continued in favor of his long-running Technic Civilization
series, though I really don't see why the two could not be
run consecutively, as this one deals chiefly with the early
history of Earth and its first solar colonies. This particular entry in the series tells of the Order of Planetary
Engineers based on Earth's moon in the Academy of Archimedes
Crater and their attempts to terraform Ganymede and Callisto
despite fierce political opposition and the bitter racial
and religious prejudices of the Jovian colonists whom they
are trying to help. Reprinted by Ace Double Novels in 1958.

Walton, Bryce: TOO LATE FOR ETERNITY (Spring, 1955)
        In this issue because of continuing   (1918-   )
economic difficulties, Startling Stories was combined with
its two companion magazines, Thrilling Wonder Stories and
Fantastic Story Magazine, and stories of increasingly
shorter length were featured. Walton's story, which was the
lead story in this issue, was described as a novel, but
twenty-eight pages constitutes at most a fairly long
novelette to me. Walton's basic premise is a very interesting one, that of an increasing disparity in the future between male and female longevity and its far-reaching effects
upon human civilization, customs and morals, but he really
needed much more length to develop his ideas to their ful-
lest extent. As it is, this "novel" is barely started
before it is over and the suffering, aged male protagonist
meets his final reward in a callous, selfish, hedonistic
world dominated by perpetually youthful and immortal
females.

Leinster, Murray: WHITE SPOT (Summer, 1955)
        This 24-page novelette by the old maestro is the
closest thing to a novel in this next to the last issue of
Startling Stories, but it is a good one, containing all the
good old-fashioned ingredients of adventure, action and
sense of wonder that characterized even the least of this

author's writings. Leinster may never have been particularly profound but he was always entertaining, and
thinking of his "Lonely Planet" novella in Thrilling Wonder
Stories of the late Forties. I would qualify that statement. In that instance, at least, he was nearly as profound
as Stanislaw Lem in Solaris on a similar subject besides
writing a much more lively and sympathetic style. Anyway,
this White Spot is a fine example of his enjoyable style,
old fashioned space opera with a shipful of terrestrials
marooned on a strange and hostile planet with a homicidal
maniac, semi-intelligent furry bipeds that love to have
their tummies scratched, and a giant heat-ray that lashes
out more or less automatically whenever any human mechanism
ventures within range.

Gunn, James L: THE NAKED SKY (Fall, 1955)   (1923-   )
     In the very last issue of Startling Stories, by the
creator of The Immortals and This Fortress World, an
intriguing little novella about a pleasure-loving, hedonistic civilization on Venus seeking to re-establish contact
with Mother Earth and the other colonies, and to discover
whether or not the mysterious Duplicates that have been ap-
pearing in the midst of humanity lately have taken over the
rest of the Solar System. This was later combined with two
other short novels, The Unhappy Man (Fantastic Universe,
February, 1955), and Name Your Pleasure (Thrilling Wonder
Stories, Winter, 1955), to form the novel, The Joy Makers,
first issued in paperback by Bantam in 1961, and then in
hardcover by Gollancz, London, in 1963. The Joy Makers was
later reprinted in hardcover by Crown Publishers, New York,
in 1984, as part of their new science fiction Classics
Series.   ▲

     And there, a long last, you have the entire roster of
the redoubtable NOVELS OF STARTLING STORIES, as they appeared from the premier issue in January, 1939, to its closing issue in the fall of 1955. I hope you have enjoyed
reading about them half as much as I have enjoyed reliving
these earliest moments of this long personal journey through
the kaleidoscopic world of Science Fiction Fantasy. This
has been a highly personalized view of what has always been
my own personal favorite science fiction magazine, and I
make no apologies for any critiques of authors or comments
on novels and plots. Not everyone will agree on what I have
said about half the stories I have mentioned or dredged out
of undeserved oblivion, or even agree that Startling Stories
was a first-rate science fiction magazine, living continually in the shadow of Astounding and Galaxy as it was,

to whose competition, among other things, it finally succumbed, but that is all to the good. The best thing about this field is that everyone can voice his opinions and speak his mind as he sees fit, and if someone doesn't like what he says, they can issue a rebuttal statement, or ignore him altogether.

I hope this book will cause some of you to look up some of these stories, if you can still find them, either in their original magazine appearances, or in their various paperback and hardcover reprints. I have tried to track them down as thoroughly as possible, primarily with the aid of Reginald's masterly Science Fiction and Fantasy Literature and Tuck's very useful first two volumes of his Encyclopedia of Science Fiction and Fantasy. Extensive revisions in this part of the text were suggested in large part by book dealer and enthusiastic fantasist, Robert Weinberg, to whom much thanks. It was one of my major objectives in setting all these words down on paper, to stimulate interest in the science fiction readers of the early eighties in these grand old stories of three or four decades earlier: that and the vicarious pleasure of experiencing again the vivid joy of reading these novels that I have always loved so much, by authors whom I likewise loved and respected all my life. I hope I have succeeded in entertaining all of you who have perused this account to some greater or lesser extent. Writing this book has been for me in every sense of the word a true labor of love.

The novels were my major interest in <u>Startling Stories</u>
when reading it in my youth, but with the passing years and
much mature reflection upon the matter, I have come to real-
ize that there were very many shorter pieces in these pages
of considerable merit, deserving at least an honorable mention in this delineation of the literary repertoire of this
excellent magazine that in so many ways epitomized the sense
of wonder that must always be at the heart and core of all
really good science fiction. It is to a survey of these
items of lesser import that I wish to devote the remaining
pages of this study.

THE SHORTS

JANUARY, 1939   VOL. 1. NO. 1.
<u>Sharp, D. D</u>: THE ETERNAL MAN   Short story.
        Immortal man story with a unique ironic twist. Hall
of Fame classic reprinted from <u>Science Wonder</u>, August, 1929.
A sequel was <u>The Eternal Man Revives</u> (<u>Wonder Story
Quarterly</u>, Summer, 1930); both were reprinted combined in
<u>The Eternal Man</u> in <u>Wonder Story Annual</u>, 1950
<u>Binder, Eando</u>: Science Island   Short story.
        Robot-controlled island utopia goes sour--as usual.
Cover artist: H. V. Brown (<u>Science Island</u>)
Editor: Mort Weisinger

MARCH, 1939   VOL. 1. NO. 2.
<u>Miller, P. Schuyler</u>: THE MAN FROM MARS   Short story.
        Morally superior Martian runs afoul of the vagaries of
human behavior. Hall of Fame classic reprinted from <u>Wonder
Stories Quarterly</u>, Summer, 1931.
<u>Hamilton, Edmond</u>: THE FEAR NEUTRALIZER   Short story.
        More messing about with glands, with somewhat less
than desirable results.
<u>Garth, Will</u>: TURNABOUT   Short story.
        Cute one-pager about blindness and the moons of
Saturn.
Cover artist: Unknown (<u>The Impossible World</u>)
Editor: Mort Weisinger

MAY, 1939   VOL. 1. NO. 3.
<u>Weinbaum, Stanley G</u>: PYGMALION'S SPECTACLES   Short story.
        Magic spectacles afford a brief glimpse into the elfin
shadowland of Paracosma-maybe. Hall of Fame classic
reprinted from <u>Wonder Stories</u>, June, 1935.
<u>Samalman, Alexander</u>: THE LOST HOUR   Short story.
        For want of an hour a dictatorship was lost.
Cover artist: H. V. Brown (<u>The Prisoner of Mars</u>)

Editor: Mort Weisinger

JULY, 1939   VOL. 2. NO. 1.
Friend, Oscar J: ROBOT A-1   Short story.
    Robot on trial for its life runs amok, with a predict-
able ending.
Sloat, Edwin K: WORLD WITHOUT NAME   Short story.
    Vintage alien invasion story, of some historical in-
terest. Hall of Fame classic reprinted from Wonder Stories,
March, 1931.
Binder, Eando: THE LIFE BATTERY   Short story.
    Neat little item about how to harness the energy of
life itself, and the results thereof.
Cover artist: H. V. Brown (Robot A-1)
Editor: Mort Weisinger

SEPTEMBER, 1939   VOL. 2. NO. 2.
Arthur, Robert: COSMIC STAGE   Short story.
    A stage magician inadvertently makes contact with
lupine invaders from an alien universe, with totally unex-
pected results. Not bad; from a real pro.
Fearn, John Russell: THE MISTY WILDERNESS   Short story.
    Future cops and robbers in the wilds of far Uranus.
Hamilton, Edmond: THE SPACE VISITORS   Short story.
    A real gem of a classic by the old master about space
fishermen who come trawling their nets for humanity,
reprinted from Air Wonder Stories, March, 1930.
Cover artist: Unknown (contest cover)
Editor: Mort Weisinger

NOVEMBER, 1939   VOL. 2. NO. 3.
Eshbach, Lloyd Arthur: THREE WISE MEN   Short story.
    Another so-so story with a reasonably predictable
trick ending.
Weinbaum, Stanley G: A MARTIAN ODYSSEY   Novelette
    Hall of Fame classic reprinted from Wonder Stories,
July, 1935. One of the first stories in the field to depict
believable and sympathetic aliens.
Cover artist: Unknown (The Fortress of Utopia)
Editor: Mort Weisinger

JANUARY, 1940   VOL. 3. NO. 1.
Friend, Oscar J: MIND OVER MATTER   Short story.
    Martian invaders become telepathic sideshow freaks.
Cover artist: H. V. Brown (Mind Over Matter)
Editor: Mort Weisinger

MARCH, 1940   VOL. 3. NO. 2.

Olsen, Bob: THE PHANTOM TELEVIEW   Short story.
     Trying to avert disaster via the medium of what was a
fantastic new invention when this story was written. Hall
of Fame classic reprinted from Science Wonder Stories,
November, 1929.
Friend, Oscar J: STATION DEATH   Short story.
     Another man-made monster unleashed upon a long-
suffering world.
Bester, Alfred: GUINEA PIG, Ph.D.   Short story.
     An early effort by this fine author, wherein a biology
professor becomes the guinea pig for experiments by alien
students.
Cover artist: H. V. Brown (Station Death)
Editor: Mort Weisinger

MAY, 1940   VOL. 3. NO. 3.
Weinbaum, Stanley G: THE VALLEY OF DREAMS   Novelette
     Further adventures on Mars with Tweel, the unforget-
table bird-man, and the deadly, insidious dream-beasts that
trap and kill by illusion. Sequel to A Martian Odyssey,
reprinted from Wonder Stories, November, 1934.
Friend, Oscar J: GLAMOUR GIRL--2040   Short story.
     Show biz of the future--big deal.
Gallun, Raymond Z: NEMESIS FROM LILLIPUT   Short story.
     An influence from the microcosmos uses an innocent
child as an unsuspecting instrument for murder.
Cover artist: H. V. Brown (Twice in Time)
Editor: Mort Weisinger

JULY, 1940   VOL. 4. NO. 1.
Manning, Laurence & Pratt, Fletcher: CITY OF THE LIVING
DEAD   Novelette
     Hall of Fame classic that first appeared in Science
Wonder Stories, May, 1930. A fine story that reads well
even today, perhaps one of the first literary examples of
world-wide media addiction, the prelude to Manning's justly
famed series of The Man Who Awoke stories.
Friend, Oscar J: THE WORMS TURN   Short story.
     Sequel to Mind Over Matter. The Martian misfits save
humanity from a mad scientist's machinations, without its
ever being aware of the fact.
Cover artist: Earle Bergey (The Worms Turn)
Editor: Mort Weisinger

SEPTEMBER, 1940   VOL. 4. NO. 2.
Herbert, Benson: THE WORLD WITHOUT   Short story.
     Hall of Fame reprint from Wonder Stories, February,
1931, that was probably the Fantastic Voyage of its day.

Cummings, Ray: THE MACHINE THAT HAD NO FLAWS   Short story.
     The title says it all—except that, of course, it did!
Bowman, Gerald: KINGDOM OF THE ANTS   Short story.
     Giant, intelligent ants in an unexplored region of
northern Australia.
Cover artist: Earle Bergey (The Kid From Mars)
Editor: Mort Weisinger

NOVEMBER, 1940   VOL. 4. NO. 3.
Ayre, Thornton: ISLAND IN THE MARSH   Short story.
     Ornithologist solves a Venusian mystery, complete with
murder.
Hamilton, Edmond: THE MAN WHO EVOLVED   Short story.
     Hall of Fame classic story of the ironic ending to a
scientist's intense quest for the ultimate goal to human
evolution, first appeared in Wonder Stories, April, 1931.
Cover artist: Earle Bergey (A Million Years To Conquer)
Editor: Mort Weisinger

JANUARY, 1941   VOL. 5. NO. 1.
Eshbach, Lloyd Arthur: THE HYPER SENSE   Short story.
     Scientific experiments give man an unwanted extra
sense—the fourth-dimensional ability to perceive the fu-
ture.
Smith, Clark Ashton: THE CITY OF THE SINGING FLAME
                                             Short story.
     Justly famed short classic about that wondrous, other-
dimensional city where myriad alien beings of diverse kinds
and races answer the hypnotic lure of the Singing Flame.
Reprinted from Wonder Stories, July, 1931.
Brackett, Leigh: THE DEMONS OF DARKSIDE   Short story.
     Interplanetary adventure on Mercury, by the wife of
Edmond Hamilton.
Cover artist: Earle Bergey (A Yank at Valhalla)
Editor: Mort Weisinger

MARCH, 1941   VOL. 5. NO. 2.
Weinbaum, Stanley G: THE WORLDS OF IF   Short story.
     Hall of Fame reprint of some of the bizarre exploits
of the irascible and very eccentric scientist, van Manderpootz, that first appeared in Wonder Stories, August, 1935.
Arthur, Robert: THE ETERNAL MOMENT   Short story.
     The strange affects of time travel on love, jealousy
and—murder!
Coblentz, Stanton A: OVER THE SPACE-WAVES   Short story.
     The swaggering bullies of giant Jupiter learn the hard
way that the so-called minor planets are not always to be
despised with safety.

Cover artist: Earle Bergey (<u>Sojarr of Titan</u>)
Editor: Mort Weisinger

MAY, 1941   VOL. 5. NO. 3.
<u>Fearn, John Russell</u>: SUPERHUMAN   Short story.
    A pair of 100-foot human giants terrorize humanity,
precursor of fifties' horror flicks.
<u>Brackett, Leigh</u>: INTERPLANETARY REPORTER   Short story.
    Cynical newsman of 2504 has his faith in humanity
rekindled by a Martian girl.
<u>Keller, Dr. David H</u>: THE LITERARY CORKSCREW   Short story.
    Rather unusual story of a writer who must undergo ex-
treme physical torment to stimulate his creative urge. Hall
of Fame classic that first appeared in <u>Wonder Stories,</u>
March, 1934.
Cover artist: Rudolph Belarski (<u>The Water World</u>)
Editor: Mort Weisinger

JULY, 1941   VOL. 6. NO. 1.
<u>Moravsky, Maria</u>: CALLING OF THE HARP   Short story.
    Bizarre story about time travel and harps--almost more
fantasy than science fiction.
<u>Morrison, William</u>: CROSSROADS OF THE UNIVERSE Short story.
    Adventure and intrigue at the Second Interplanetary
Fair, held on the artificial planetoid of Neonia--shadows of
Alfred Hitchcock!
<u>Jones, Ralph T</u>: THE MAN-BEAST OF TOREE   Novelette
    Interesting reprint from <u>Wonder Stories,</u> July, 1931,
about the far world of Toree where humans are deprived of
their thumbs and kept as pets and beasts of burden by unsympathetic aliens.
Cover artist: Rudolph Belarski (<u>Gateway To Paradise</u>)
Editor: Oscar J. Friend

SEPTEMBER, 1941   VOL. 6. NO. 2.
<u>Hilliard, A. Rowley</u>: DEATH FROM THE STARS   Short story.
    A real chiller of a science fiction horror story about
an insidious, invisible death that infects humanity from an
ancient meteor. Real Hall of Fame classic from <u>Wonder
Stories,</u> October, 1931. A sequel was a novelette, <u>Reign of
the Star-Death</u>, printed in <u>Wonder Stories</u>, April, 1932, but
never reprinted, as far as I can tell.
<u>Long, Frank Belknap</u>: PRISONERS IN FLATLAND   Short story.
    Interplanetary adventures in the Asteroid Belt.
<u>Williams, Robert Moore</u>: NO HEROES WANTED   Short story.
    The tables are turned on a spaceship test pilot--a
spaceship tests him!
Cover artist: Rudolph Belarski (<u>The Bottom of the World</u>)

Editor: Oscar J. Friend

NOVEMBER, 1941   VOL. 6. NO. 3.
Bloch, Robert: LAST LAUGH   Short story.
     Grisly little item about bodiless heads, headless
bodies and revenge--science fiction style.
Keller, Dr. David H: THE BONELESS HORROR   Short story.
     Hall of Fame classic about the true story behind the
legends of Atlantis and Mu, and the war that destroyed the
first great civilization of mankind. Reprinted from Science
Wonder Stories, July, 1929.
Broome, John: TRAIL'S END   Short story.
     Science fiction morality tale.
Cover artist: Rudolph Belarski (The Gods Hate Kansas)
Editor: Oscar J. Friend

JANUARY, 1942   VOL. 7. NO. 1.
Asimov, Isaac: CHRISTMAS ON GANYMEDE   Short story.
     Early science fiction by this justly famed old master
of the genre; humorous satire about bringing the blessings
of Christmas to the benighted heathen denizens of Jupiter's
moon.
Breuer, M.D., Dr. Miles J: THE FITZGERALD CONTRACTION
                                          Short story.
     Interesting classic reprint about the bizarre effects
of relativity on space and time and humanity that first appeared in Science Wonder Stories, January, 1930. A sequel
of sorts was The Time Flight (Amazing Stories, June, 1931).
Gallun, Raymond Z: GEARS FOR NEMESIS   Short story.
     Mystery and sabotage on the hostile planet of Nemesis.
Cover artist: Rudolph Belarski (Devil's Planet)
Editor: Oscar J. Friend

MARCH, 1942   VOL. 7. NO. 2.
Kuttner, Henry: SILENT EDEN   Short story.
     Two mortals trapped in a superhuman alien's private
universe.
Starzl, R. F: HORNETS OF SPACE   Short story.
     So-so mini-epic of the I.F.P.'s struggle to keep the
space lanes free for commerce and civilization, and how a
supposed coward eventually proved his worth to them. Hall
of Fame classic reprinted from Wonder Stories, November,
1930.
Millard, Joseph J: MISTER JOHN DOE, EARTHMAN Short story.
     Amnesiac alien tries to save Earth from being snuffed
by deadly cosmic cloud.
Cover artist: Earle Bergey (Tarnished Utopia)
Editor: Oscar J. Friend

MAY, 1942   VOL. 7. NO. 3.
Lewis, Richard O: ALLA-BEG'S GENII   Short story.
    Crooked stage magician trifles with alien beings in
another dimension, to his regret.
Maddocks, G. L: MACROCOSMIC   Short story.
    Scientific investigator absorbs his universe when he
visits the macrocosmos above.
Coblentz, Stanton A: THE MAKING OF MISTY ISLE Short story.
    Interesting reprint from Science Wonder Stories, June,
1929, of how unscrupulous men's unwise tampering with nature
disastrously backfired upon them.
Cover artist: Earle Bergey (Blood on the Sun)
Editor: Oscar J. Friend

JULY, 1942   VOL. 8. NO. 1.
McDowd, Kennie: THE MARBLE VIRGIN   Short story.
    Modern science fiction version of the Pygmalion story,
reprinted from Science Wonder Stories, June, 1929. This one
they could have skipped.
Morrison, William: THE MAN IN THE MOON   Short story.
    Intended benefactor of mankind is clobbered because he
is non-human. Ironic.
Hansen, L. Taylor: THE GHOST SHIP OF ATZLAN   Short story.
    Very interesting little story of a ghost ship in the
Sargasso Sea, with lost race overtones and scientific ex-
planations for ghostly phenomena of the sea.
Cover artist: Earle Bergey (Symbolic--?)
Editor: Oscar J. Friend

SEPTEMBER, 1942   VOL. 8. NO. 2.
Tucker, Louis: THE CUBIC CITY   Short story.
    Hall of Fame reprint from Science Wonder Stories, Sep-
tember, 1929, about how Griswold Lee mentally visited the
ultra-scientific world of the cubic cities.
Jerome, Owen Fox: METEORITE ENIGMA   Short story.
    Strange meteorite gem plunges Bob Graham's party into
an alien and deadly world.
Johnson, Frank: KIDS DIDN'T KNOW EVERYTHING   Short story.
    Old-time spaceman teaches quiz kids of the future a
few things.
Cover artist: Rudolph Belarski (Meteorite Enigma)
Editor: Oscar J. Friend

NOVEMBER, 1942   VOL. 8. NO. 3.
Millard, Joseph J: THE EARTH-SAVER   Short story.
Under-average schmo saves the world from aliens with a burp.
Ludicrous and dumb.

Strangland, A. G: THE ANCIENT BRAIN   Short story.
     Hall of Fame reprint from Science Wonder Stories, Oc-
tober, 1929. A twentieth-century brain is resurrected in a
body 10,000 years in the future. Of historical interest
only.
Lewis, Henry S: DEATH RAY   Short story.
     Meek scientist outwits Nazi spy. Barely passable fil-
ler.
Cover artist: Earle Bergey (The Day of the Cloud)
Editor: Oscar J. Friend

JANUARY, 1943   VOL. 9. NO. 1.
Morrison, William: FORGOTTEN PAST   Short story.
     History-scanning machine reviews scenes from the for-
gotten past.
Hilliard, A. Rowley: THE GREEN TORTURE   Short story.
     Interesting reprint from Wonder Stories, March, 1931.
How to break a stubborn patriot scientifically--maybe.
Nitkin, Nathaniel: THE MAN WHO WAS KING   Short story.
     Ex-space pirate turns hero to save Martian colony from
a deadly plague.
Dennis, Walt & Tucker, Ernest: THE GLADIATORS Short story.
     Surprisingly good story about the gladiatorial games
that make life bearable for the People of the Domes, trapped
in their shelters by a polluted environment, and the heroic
men who wage them. With an ending reminiscent of Logan's
Run.
Cover artist: Rudolph Belarski (World Beyond the Sky)
Editor: Oscar J. Friend

MARCH, 1943   VOL. 9. NO. 2.
Long, Frank Belknap: THE GLORY FLIGHT   Short story.
     Sentient red crystals inhabiting Saturn's Crepe Ring
attempt to control human minds.
Morrison, William: THE GREAT INVASION   Short story.
     Mutual misunderstandings threaten to turn mankind's
first meeting with an alien race into a tragedy.
Carpenter, S. C: THE SUPER VELOCITOR   Short story.
     Hall of Fame classic; reprinted from Science Wonder
Stories, December, 1929. Probably one of the first stories
to describe machine enabling humans to live at different
rates of speed than normal.
Cover artist: Earle Bergey (Speak of the Devil)
Editor: Oscar J. Friend

JUNE, 1943   VOL. 9. NO. 3.
Weinbaum, Stanley G: THE IDEAL   Short story.
     Mildly amusing van Manderpootz story reprinted from

Wonder Stories, September, 1935, wherein the eccentric inventor attempts to devise a brain for his ideal machine, the mechanical carnivore!

Long, Frank Belknap: SON OF HIS FATHER   Short story.
     Trials and tribulations of an Earthling schoolteacher on Io.

Gallun, Raymond Z: HELL-STUFF FOR PLANET X   Short story.
     Old-fashioned space opera in a small dose. Heroics on Mercury's Twilight Zone.

Lee, Thorn: GHOST PLANET   Short story.
     Invisible pirates ravage the inhabitants of the United Planets.

Cover artist: Earle Bergey (Wings of Icarus)
Editor: Oscar J. Friend

FALL, 1943   VOL. 10. NO. 1.
Morrison, William: THE MONKEY AND THE TYPEWRITER
                                               Short story.
     Instantaneous matter transmission by radio, accidentally.

Gallun, Raymond Z: THE SPACE DWELLERS   Short story.
     Hall of Fame classic that first appeared in Science Wonder Stories, November, 1929, about an alien life-form that thrives in the cold and rigors of outer space.

Farrell, Joseph: SECRET WEAPON   Short story.
     Short story about how to outwit an extraordinarily powerful and ruthless space pirate.

Cover artist: Earle Bergey (Pirates of the Time Trail)
Editor: Oscar J. Friend

WINTER, 1944   VOL. 10. NO. 2.
Gardner, Thomas S: THE LAST WOMAN   Short story.
     First published in Wonder Stories, April, 1932, this Hall of Fame classic describes the tragic end of the last surviving woman after Earthmen have learned how to do without them.

Rocklynne, Ross: BEYOND THE BOILING ZONE   Short story.
     Visiting the mythical planet Vulcan, to find it two-dimensional!

Kuttner, Henry: MUSIC HATH CHARMS   Short story.
     Detectives and murder in the twenty-second century, on the pleasure planet of Sky City.

Coblentz, Stanton A: SIDEREAL TIME-BOMB   Short story.
     Explosive danger to Earth from a lost relic planet of a vanished, extra-Solar race.

Cover artist: Earle Bergey (The Giant Atom)
Editor: Oscar J. Friend

SPRING, 1944   VOL. 10. NO. 3.
Jacobi, Carl: CANAL   Short story.
     Very entertaining cops and robbers chase story on
Mars.
Weinbaum, Stanley G: THE POINT OF VIEW   Short story.
     Hall of Fame classic reprinted from Wonder Stories,
January, 1936, about van Manderpootz's somewhat bizarre ex-
periments with cosmology and psychology.
Long, Frank Belknap: SPAWN OF THE FURTHER DARK Short story.
     Hitch-hiking in space with strangers can be a risky
business!
Farrell, Joseph: THE BARD OF CERES   Short story.
     Space pirates and Shakespeare on an asteroid world.
Cover artist: Earle Bergey (The Great Ego)
Editor: Oscar J. Friend

SUMMER, 1944   VOL. 11. NO. 1.
Morrison, William: GET YOUR EXTRA, HERE!   Short story.
     Hen-pecked husband finds adventure--and guts--in
another world.
Cross, Polton: WANDERER OF TIME   Short story.
     To escape the electric chair, Blake Corson wills him-
self into the future.
Smith, Ford: THE SERUM RUBBER MAN   Short story.
     Scientific experimentation turns a human into a real
india-rubber man.
Smith, Clark Ashton: BEYOND THE SINGING FLAME   Novelette.
     The final answer to what befell the entranced victims
of the Singing Flame after their self-immolation, reprinted
from Wonder Stories, November, 1931.
Cover artist: Earle Bergey (Strangers on the Heights)
Editor: Oscar J. Friend

FALL, 1944   VOL. 11. NO. 2.
Jacobi, Carl: THE COSMIC DOODLER   Short story.
     A man's doodlings become the key to discovery of
humanity's lost interstellar origins.
Sharp, D. D: THE DAY OF THE BEAST   Short story.
     Creation of a biological monstrosity by unwise scien-
tific experimentation with insects and spiders, reprinted
from Science Wonder Stories, May, 1930.
Chute, Verne: THE MAD DOMNEYS   Short story.
     Fantasy about an average American family disrupted by
appearance of a cat named Cecil.
Stoddard, Charles: THE INVISIBLE VANDALS   Short story.
     More space pirates, and how they outsmart themselves--
again!
Cover artist: Earle Bergey (Shadow Over Mars)

Editor: Sam Merwin, Jr.

WINTER, 1945   VOL. 11. NO. 3.
Long, Frank Belknap: DARK COMMAND   Short story.
        Space patrol encounters witchcraft on Mars. Not bad,
for this author.
Gleason, C. Sterling: THE RADIATION OF THE CHINESE VEGETABLE
        Not-so-classic reprint from   Short story.
Science Wonder Stories, December, 1929, that is a very inept
spoof of early science fiction in general and the yellow
peril type story in particular.
Northern, Leslie: SKYROVER   Short story.
        Faithful Rover saves the day on Jupiter's moon. Noth-
ing much.
Smith, Ford: THE COSMIC CHAIN   Short story.
        One writer's answer to the mystery behind our expand-
ing universe. Interesting.
Cover artist: Earle Bergey (Iron Men)
Editor: Sam Merwin, Jr.

SPRING, 1945   VOL. 12. NO. 1.
Smith, Ford: ARE YOU THERE, CHARLIE?   Short story.
        Herman Cattlehop receives financial advice from an
extra-dimensional visitor--with three legs.
Jameson, Malcolm: DEATH BY PROXY   Short story.
        Another Axis spy gets his comeuppance through the
medium of advanced science.
Hamilton, Edmond: THE ISLAND OF UNREASON   Short story.
        Reprinted from Wonder Stories, May, 1933, this very
readable story tells of the island where misfits and incor-
rigibles are isolated from civilization in the future.
Cover artist: Earle Bergey (Red Sun of Danger)
Editor: Sam Merwin, Jr.

SUMMER, 1945   VOL. 12. NO. 2.
Repp, Ed Earl: THE RED DIMENSION   Short story.
        Murder is committed in Russia by a creature from
another dimension. Not-so-hot Hall of Fame classic (?) that
first appeared in Science Wonder Stories, January, 1930.
Northern, Leslie: FATAL THOUGHTS   Short story.
        A man's subconscious hate battles an alien beast. Not
bad for a filler.
Cover artist: Earle Bergey (The Hollow World)
Editor: Sam Merwin, Jr.

FALL, 1945   VOL. 12. NO. 3.
Leinster, Murray: INCIDENT ON CALYPSO   Short story.
        Stranded Earthman finds help from sympathetic robots

of an alien race.

Flagg, Francis: THE SUPERMAN OF DR. JUKES   Novelette.
     Fast-paced story about an artificially created physi-
cal superman who is also a master criminal, now seeking
revenge on double-crossing crooked politicians and mobsters.
Hall of Fame classic reprinted from Wonder Stories, November, 1931.

Hamilton, Edmond: TROUBLE ON TRITON   Short story.
     Good old-fashioned space opera by the master prac-
titioner of the genre.

Cover artist: Earle Bergey (Aftermath)
Editor: Sam Merwin, Jr.

WINTER, 1946   VOL. 13. NO. 1.

Miller, P. Schuyler: THE FORGOTTEN MAN OF SPACE Short story.
     Poignant, pathetic story of the abandoned hermit
Earthman of Mars, and of man's cruel, callous inhumanity to
man. Great reprint story from Wonder Stories, April, 1933.

Merwin, Jr., Sam: THE JIMSON ISLAND GIANT   Short story.
     About a man who literally got too big for his
britches--and his world.

Cover artist: Earle Bergey (Outlaw World)
Editor: Sam Merwin, Jr.

MARCH, 1946   VOL. 13. NO. 2.

Long, Frank Belknap: SHADOW OVER VENUS   Short story.
     Domination of human minds by the sinister Venusian
gules. Sound familiar?

Williamson, Jack: TWELVE HOURS TO LIVE   Short story.
     Interesting science fiction variant of the classic
psychological puzzle tale of Frank R. Stockton's, The Lady
or the Tiger, complete with sinister space pirate and a
deadly, devouring fungus. First published in Wonder
Stories, August, 1931.

Kuttner, Henry: THE DARK ANGEL   Short story.
     Another of this author's fascinating stories about su-
perior mutant humans born so far ahead of their proper
evolutionary time that they become monsters in our normal
world.

Cover artist: Earle Bergey (Valley of the Flame)
Editor: Sam Merwin, Jr.

SPRING, 1946   VOL. 13. NO. 3.

Smith, Clark Ashton: THE DIMENSION OF CHANCE   Novelette.
     Really bizarre story about a world in an alien dimen-
sion where biological consistency of shape, race and form is
dictated wholly by chance, accidentally visited by Jap-
hunting Americans engaged in a Sino-American war in 1975,

first printed in Wonder Stories, November, 1932.
Hamilton, Edmond: THE DEAD PLANET   Short story.
     A good one about aliens who discover the lost planet
of Earth, guarded by its dead.
Fearn, John Russell: THE UNBROKEN CHAIN   Short story.
     Wonderfully imaginative story about a future savant's
quest through many lives for knowledge with which to combat
the malignant Ice Life that is destroying his world.
Cover artist: Earle Bergey (Other Eyes Watching)
Editor: Sam Merwin, Jr.

SUMMER, 1946   VOL. 14. NO. 1.
Hamilton, Edmond: THE MAN WITH X-RAY EYES   Short story.
     One of the old master's excellent psychological
studies, about what it would be like for an ordinary man to
become suddenly possessed of an extraordinary power. First
appeared in Wonder Stories, November, 1933.
Vance, Jack: PLANET OF THE BLACK DUST   Short story.
     Vintage Vance about how an honest spaceman outwits
pirates on an alien world.
Cross, Polton: THE VICIOUS CIRCLE   Short story.
     Earthman becomes human pendulum in time--precursor of
"The Seesaw" in van Vogt's Weapon Shops series.
Rocklynne, Ross: EXTRA EARTH   Short story.
     One of those stories about a duplicate Earth on the
other side of the Sun.
Cover artist: Earle Bergey (The Dark World)
Editor: Sam Merwin, Jr.

FALL, 1946   VOL. 14. NO. 2.
Flagg, Francis: AFTER ARMAGEDDON   Short story.
     Better-than-average fall of civilization and post-
catastrophe story that first appeared in Wonder Stories,
September, 1932.
Thiessen, W. E: AFRAID   Short story.
     Norman Kane braves the mental terrors that are the
weapons of the Moon's inhabitants.
Kuttner, Henry: ABSALOM   Short story.
     Another story of a super-mutant child, as only Kuttner
could write them. .
Cover artist: Earle Bergey (The Solar Invasion)
Editor: Sam Merwin, Jr.

JANUARY, 1947 .   VOL. 14. NO. 3.
Schachner, Nathan & Zagat, Arthur Leo: VENUS MINES, INCOR-
PORATED   Novelette.
     Readable space opera about humans vs. giant green Mar-
tians by this talented team of old-time collaborators,

reprinted from Wonder Stories, August, 1931.
Leinster, Murray: FRIENDS   Short story.
    Telepathic twins foil the plans of military dictators
for World War.
Whetly, George: TRAVELER'S TALE   Short story.
    Time traveler finds the future--or past--is not quite
what he had expected.
Cover artist: Earle Bergey (The Star of Life)
Editor: Sam Merwin, Jr.

MARCH, 1947   VOL. 15. NO. 1.
Wellman, Manly Wade: WHEN PLANETS CLASHED   Novelette.
    Hall of Fame War of the Worlds story by this in-
defatigable old-timer first appeared in Wonder Stories
Quarterly, Spring, 1931. Superior.
St. Clair, Margaret: THE SOMA RACKS   Short story.
    First of the Oona and Jick stories, about a housewife
of the future and her long-suffering hubby, whom she doses
with her vitalizers in this one to cure him of lethargy.
Barrett, John: STELLAR SNOWBALL   Short story.
    Pirates and stowaways keep a spaceship hopping.
Cover artist: Rudolph Belarski (The Laws of Chance)
Editor: Sam Merwin, Jr.

MAY, 1947   VOL. 15. NO. 2.
Wellman, Manly Wade: THE DISC-MEN OF JUPITER   Novelette.
    Sequel to When Planets Clashed, first printed in
Wonder Stories, September, 1931. Martians and Terrestrials
join forces to explore unknown giant Jupiter and run afoul
of a woman's caprices and the hostility of a totally alien
species.
Heinlein, Robert A: COLUMBUS WAS A DOPE   Short story.
    Pleasant short short about bartending on the Moon.
Fearn, John Russell: THE ARBITER   Short story.
    Thoughtful, ironic story about the dangers of delegat-
ing human responsibility for justice and morality to
machines.
Cover artist: Earle Bergey (The Disc-Men of Jupiter)
Editor: Sam Merwin, Jr.

JULY, 1947   VOL. 15. NO. 3.
Binder, Otto: THE RING BONANZA   Short story.
    Space prospector strikes it rich in Saturn's Rings,
but there are still claim jumpers even in the future.
Keller, David H: THE LIFE DETOUR   Short story.
    Hall of Fame classic reprinted from Wonder Stories,
February, 1935, about elitist politics of the future and how
differences in class were finally resolved by a simple

57

changing of--water.

Kuttner, Henry: DREAM'S END   Short story.
        Neat psychological fantasy about dreams within dreams
within dreams within--

Hamilton, Edmond: PROXY PLANETEERS   Short story.
        Robot proxies explore hostile Mercury for Earthling
scientists, unaware of indigenous intelligent life-forms
that have a thing or two to say about this invasion.

St. Clair, Margaret: SUPER WHOST   Short story.
        Future housewife Oona and her hubby, Jick, run afoul
of the devious machinations of breakfast food contests
promising a free trip to Mars if--

Cover artist: Earle Bergey (The Kingdom of the Blind)
Editor: Sam Merwin, Jr.

SEPTEMBER, 1947   VOL. 16. NO. 1.

Weinbaum, Stanley G: THE CIRCLE OF ZERO   Novelette.
        Interesting reprint story from Thrilling Wonder
Stories, August, 1936, whose ending can be interpreted in
either of two ways, actual glimpses of alternate realities
that have already occurred or simple mental aberration and
self-delusion.

Jacobi, Carl: LODANA   Short story.
        Goddess of Jupiter's Sixth Moon prevents an uprising
of the Mutant laborers.

Cummings, Ray: UP AND ATOM   Short story.
        More of the adventures of Tubby, a long-running series
by this old-time writer that were simply sugar-coated (?)
gems of scientific wisdom. Barely palatable for modern
tastes.

Cover artist: Earle Bergey (Lord of the Atom--symbolic
presentation)
Editor: Sam Merwin, Jr.

NOVEMBER, 1947   VOL. 16. NO. 2.

Williamson, Jack: THROUGH THE PURPLE CLOUD   Short story.
        Murder and madness results when a passenger plane
takes an unscheduled journey into an alien world through a
purple cloud, reprinted from Wonder Stories, May, 1931. Far
below par for the creator of The Legion of Space series and
other acknowledged classics.

Cross, Polton: CHAOS   Short story.
        Another fictional answer to the legend of lost Atlan-
tis.

Beck, Clyde: ANASTOMOSIS   Short story.
        Exploring more than four dimensions entails certain
risks--

Cover artist: Earle Bergey (Through the Purple Cloud)

Editor: Sam Merwin, Jr.

JANUARY, 1948   VOL. 16. NO. 3.
Hamilton, Edmond: THE CONQUEST OF TWO WORLDS , Novelette.
   Hall of Fame classic reprinted from Wonder Stories, February, 1932. Tragic account of Earthmen's ruthless exploitation, brutalization and conquest of the less highly evolved inhabitants of Mars and Jupiter, obviously based upon our historical treatment of the Indians.
St. Clair, Margaret: ALEPH SUB ONE   Short story.
   Oona and Jick mess around with a too-smart robot calculator, almost to the world's sorrow.
Cross, Polton: ULTRA EVOLUTION   Short story.
   Another interesting speculation about what might be the ultimate evolution of Man.
Evans, E. Everett: GUARANTEED   Short story.
   Cute one-pager about an unsatisfied customer from one million years hence.
Cover artist: Earle Bergey (The Blue Flamingo)
Editor: Sam Merwin, Jr.

MARCH, 1948   VOL. 17. NO. 1.
Weinbaum, Stanley G: THE BRINK OF INFINITY Short story.
   Hall of Fame classic reprinted from Thrilling Wonder Stories, December, 1936. About the only story I ever read that made abstruse higher mathematics interesting to me. Combination puzzle story and thriller. Maybe a little crude, but good.
Long, Frank Belknap: AND WE SAILED THE MIGHTY DARK
               Novelette.
   Lucky Jim acquires strange shipmates when he finds the Graveyard of Lost Ships.
Kuttner, Henry: DON'T LOOK NOW   Short story.
   What not to do if a three-eyed Martian is spying on you.
Blish, James: MISTAKE INSIDE   Short story.
   Unknown-type fantasy about Hugh Tracy and his trip Outside to—where?
Sprague, Carter: CLIMATE—DISORDERED   Short story.
   Changing the weather can be tricky—and dangerous to one's job.
Ettinger, R. C. W: THE PENULTIMATE TRUMP Short story.
   A ruthless tycoon who takes a long sleep to escape the consequences of his financial crimes finds that the future is not at all what he had expected.
Cover artist: Earle Bergey (One of Three)
Editor: Sam Merwin, Jr.

MAY, 1948   VOL. 17. NO. 2.
Zagat, Arthur Leo: NO ESCAPE FROM DESTINY   Novelette.
        Interesting combination of science fiction, big busi-
ness machinations and a nine-fold murder mystery by an old
master of the genre.
Cummings, Ray: THE SIMPLE LIFE   Short story.
        Escaping the complexities of civilization by fleeing
into outer space. Seems drastic.
Long, Frank Belknap: THE HOUSE OF RISING WINDS Short story.
        Modern classic about a little boy befriended by an
alien collector of dangerous beasts.
Williams, Robert Moore: THE SEEKERS   Short story.
        Masterminds of Mars find they have not discovered all
the answers, after all.
Smith, George O: JOURNEY   Short story.
        A trip to Alpha Centauri that nobody on Earth will
believe in.
Fearn, John Russell: AFTER THE ATOM   Short story.
        Ironic story of time travel, would-be peace-givers and
future human mutations.
Ernst, Paul: THE MICROSCOPIC GIANTS   Short story.
        Science fiction horror story reprinted from Thrilling
Wonder Stories, October, 1936, about murderous little men
who can move through solid rock.
Cover artist: Earle Bergey (The Mask of Circe)
Editor: Sam Merwin, Jr.

JULY, 1948   VOL. 17. NO. 3.
MacDowell, Emmett: REALITIES UNLIMITED   Novelette.
        Martian mind-trap almost snares the second expedition
to the Red Planet, but human tenacity and stubbornness prove
more than a match for the alien wiles.
Hubbard, L. Ron: WHEN SHADOWS FALL   Short story.
        One of Hubbard's better efforts, how a dying Earth was
saved not by guns or gold but by a memory and a song.
Kuttner, Henry: WHEN THE EARTH LIVED   Short story.
        Chilling reprint from Thrilling Wonder Stories, Oc-
tober, 1937, telling what happened on Earth when a shift in
the intensity of cosmic rays caused the normally inanimate
to become animate—and deadly!
Vance, Jack: HARD-LUCK DIGGINGS   Short story.
        First in the series of the fabulous exploits of Magnus
Ridolph, interstellar investigator and entrepreneur, concerning the inexplicable killings in the mines of a far-
distant planet.
St. Clair, Margaret: QUIS CUSTODIET?   Short story.
        Chilling post-catastrophe story about mutant killers
inimical to all normal life-forms.

Sheldon, Walt: PERFECT SERVANT   Short story.
    Fantasy of an obedient robot flunky from the future
who at the end of the story may be presumed to be something
much more than he at first appeared to be.   ·
Cover artist: Earle Bergey (When the Earth Lived)
Editor: Sam Merwin, Jr.

SEPTEMBER, 1948   VOL. 18. NO. 1.
Miller, P. Schuyler: TETRAHEDRA OF SPACE   Novelette.
    Hall of Fame classic that first appeared in Wonder
Stories, November, 1931, recounting the invasion of Earth in
the South American jungles by the living tetrahedra of Mercury. Better written and plotted than the average for this
sort of thing, by a writer who was once considered a second
A. Merritt. This story, by his own admission, exerted some
influence on Isaac Asimov's formative years as a writer.
De Courcy, Dorothy and John: RAT RACE   Short story.
    Interstellar politics and one-upmanship as practiced
in the not-so-far future by Earthmen and a race of ratlike
conquerors, with a mildly amusing and somewhat unexpected
trick ending.
MacDonald, John D: SHENADUN   Short story.
    Vintage science fiction from the salad days of a
modern master of the hard-boiled detective novel, about the
strange secret that lay behind the mystery of the mighty
mountain of Shenadun.
Vance, Jack: SANATORIS SHORT-CUT   Short story.
    Magnus Ridolph uses mathematics to outwit the master
space pirate, Acco May.
Cover artist: Earle Bergey (What Mad Universe--symbolic
presentation)
Editor: Sam Merwin, Jr.

NOVEMBER, 1948   VOL. 18. NO. 2.
Pragnell, Festus: THE ISOTOPE MEN   Novelette.
    Hall of Fame classic reprinted from Wonder Stories,
August, 1933, telling of the pre-birth experience of an
Earthling on the forgotten planet of the Isotope Men, whence
mankind originally migrated at the time of its destruction.
Williams, Robert Moore: THE STUBBORN MEN   Short story.
    Tragedy stalks a family of stubborn and dedicated re-
searchers in atomic physics.
Long, Frank Belknap: HUMPTY DUMPTY HAD A GREAT FALL
                                              Short story.
    Bizarre story of the other-dimensional reality behind
the Mother Goose rhymes. Macabre and grim.
van Vogt, A. E: DORMANT   Short story.
    One of van Vogt's most unforgettable early stories, of

61

Iilah the dormant death--
MacDonald, John D: RING AROUND THE REDHEAD   Short story.
     Bill Maloney is on trial for murder, and his only
defense depends on a gorgeous red-headed girl from another
world.
Bradbury, Ray: THE VISITOR   Short story.
     Life is made worth living once more for the dying
lungers of Mars by a telepathic mutant.
Vance, Jack: THE UNSPEAKABLE MCINCH   Short story.
     Magnus Ridolph has a whole plethora of bizarre
suspects to choose from for a particularly clever murderer
and thief on Sclerotto Planet.
Cover artist: Earle Bergey (Against the Fall of Night)
Editor: Sam Merwin, Jr.

JANUARY, 1949   VOL. 18. NO. 3.
Phillips, Alexander, M: MARTIAN GESTURE   Novelette.
     Well-written account of attempt by philanthropic Mar-
tians to save surviving Earthlings from the consequences of
the catastrophic war that has destroyed their civilization,
first published in Wonder Stories, October, 1935.
Vance, John D: THE SUB-STANDARD SARDINES   Novelette.
     Magnus Ridolph investigates sabotage in the sardine
cannery of Chandaria, with really unexpected results.
MacDonald, John D: FLAW   Short story.
     Tragic and unexpected results of space-travel, due to
a grossly mistaken view of our cosmos.
Leinster, Murray: THE STORY OF ROD CANTRELL   Short story.
     Rod Cantrell saves the world from would-be military
dictators, prelude to Black Galaxy.
Stockheker, R. W: THE FISSION MAN   Short story.
     Isotopic physicist achieves space travel.
Lafayette, Rene: FORBIDDEN VOYAGE   Short story.
     First of the Conquest of Space series.
Cover artist: Earle Bergey (The Time Axis)
Editor: Sam Merwin, Jr.

MARCH, 1949   VOL. 19. NO. 1.
Simak, Clifford D: THE LOOT OF TIME   Novelette.
     Excellent early Simak about a battle through time with
devilish Centaurian pirates, and of some modern human's
friendship for an elderly Neanderthaler that eventually
caused him to be worshipped as a god by his contemporaries.
First printed in Thrilling Wonder Stories, December, 1938.
Williams, Robert Moore: THE SOUND OF BUGLES   Novelette.
     Earthmen discover that the Martians have found an al-
ternative to the Biblical injunction, that by toil and labor
and by the sweat of the brow only may their living be

62

earned, one which they cannot duplicate.

Lafayette, Rene: THE MAGNIFICENT FAILURE   Short story.
        Second in the Conquest of Space series, of the brilliant dwarf who led mankind to Mars and beyond despite themselves.

Vance, Jack: THE HOWLING BOUNDERS   Short story.
        Magnus Ridolph battles to save a precious ticholama crop from destruction by seemingly invulnerable predators.

Bradbury, Ray: MARIONETTES, INC.   Short story.
        Classic early story by this fine author of a bizarre company that builds robot copies to order of anyone who can afford to pay their price, regardless of the consequences.

Loomis, Noel: TURNOVER TIME   Short story.
        Earth expedition to the Moon misses the target, but zeroes in on an invasion from Mars.

Cover artist: Earle Bergey (The Black Galaxy)

Editor: Sam Merwin, Jr.

MAY, 1949   VOL. 19. NO. 2.

Binder, Eando: CONQUEST OF LIFE
        First of the Anton York stories about the problems and ramifications resulting from the discovery of personal human body immortality, first printed in Thrilling Wonder Stories, August, 1937. In this one York wins a deathless bride and saves Earth from conquest by immortal tyrants.

Merwin, Jr., Sam: FORGOTTEN ENVOY   Novelette.
        Spy from an alien world of cyclops turns pugilist on Earth as his cover, with disastrous results for the enemy.

Lafayette, Rene: THE INCREDIBLE DESTINATION   Short story.
        Third in the Conquest of Space series, wherein James Donlon leads mankind to the stars and is regarded as a charlatan for his trouble.

Reed, Blair: DIMENSION: PRAECOX   Short story.
        The Lochwald Department Store is haunted by an inexplicably disembodied hand in broad daylight, until Officer Clancy takes a hand of his own--

MacDonald, John D: IMMORTALITY   Short story.
        Short short about the real cosmic meaning behind deja vu.

Clarke, Arthur C: HISTORY LESSON   Short story.
        Ironic little tale of how the Venusians came to have a totally erroneous conception of the true nature of their glacier-smothered human neighbors.

Cover artist: Earle Bergey (Flight Into Yesterday--symbolic presentation)

Editor: Sam Merwin, Jr.

JULY, 1949   VOL. 19. NO. 3.

St. Clair, Margaret: THE SACRED MARTIAN PIG   Novelette.
     Story of the most totally useless cult in the
Universe, and of the unwitting Earthman who became involved
with it and its somewhat eccentric votaries.
Kuttner, Henry: HOLLYWOOD ON THE MOON   Novelette.
     Hall of Fame reprint from Thrilling Wonder Stories,
April, 1938, about the bizarre exploits of Anthony Quade,
ace troubleshooter for Von Zorn, Lunar movie mogul of the
future, on Jupiter's moon and our own.
Lafayette, Rene: THE UNWILLING HERO   Short story.
     Fourth in the Conquest of Space series, of Vic Hardin
and his unwilling rise to fame and glory.
Clarke, Arthur C: TRANSIENCE   Short story.
     Poetic story of the enduring tenacity of Man and the
fleeting mortality of his worlds.
Kornbluth, C. M: THE ONLY THING WE LEARN   Short story.
     The restless barbarians return to sack the mother
world, again and again and again--
Bradbury, Ray: THE LONELY ONES   Short story.
     Two men and a woman--even a dead one--alone on Mars
can sometimes be the cause of serious complications, either
of tragedy or comedy.
Cover artist: Earle Bergey (Fire in the Heavens)
Editor: Sam Merwin, Jr.

SEPTEMBER, 1949   VOL. 20. NO. 1.
Barnes, Arthur K: THE HOTHOUSE PLANET   Novelette.
     First of the extraordinary exploits of Gerry Carlyle,
indefatigable female Frank Buck of the future, reprinted
from Thrilling Wonder Stories, October, 1937, wherein the
interplanetary huntress meets her match in the person of the
most innocuous of creatures, the Murri of Venus.
Jones, Edwin: COMMUNICATIONS   Short story.
     Communications continue to be the lifeblood of war-
fare, even interplanetary warfare.
MacDonald, John D: A CONDITION OF BEAUTY   Short story.
     Ironic story of mutations, space travel and lost
colonies, which proves that beauty is truly in the eye--and
conditioning--of the beholder.
Clarke, Arthur C: THE FIRES WITHIN   Short story.
     Who knows what terrors lurk beneath the Earth's crust,
until it is too late--?
Lafayette, Rene: BEYOND THE BLACK NEBULA   Short story.
     Penetrating the most formidable menace to interstellar
navigation known to man--the Coal Sack! Another in the Conquest of Space series.
Cover artist: Earle Bergey (The Hothouse Planet)
Editor: Sam Merwin, Jr.

NOVEMBER, 1949   VOL. 20. NO. 2.
Taine, John: THE ULTIMATE CATALYST   Novelette.
     Rather grisly tale of how a brilliant scientist
chooses to rid the world of the last of its dictators and
tyrants by transmuting them into a different form of life
altogether. Hall of Fame classic written by the famed math-
ematician, Eric Temple Bell, under his equally famous non de
plume, and first published in Thrilling Wonder Stories,
June, 1939.
Sprague, Carter: JOURNEY FOR ONE   Short story.
     Dr. Craig Buckner finds unwanted love from a woman of
the fiftieth century.
Vance, Jack: THE KING OF THIEVES   Short story.
     Magnus Ridolph nearly meets his match on Moritaba,
world of thieves, but--it does take one to know one or to
beat them at their own game.
Williams, Robert Moore: HOMEWARD BOUND   Short story.
     How many men from Mars are there on Earth anyway, and
who is really fooling who?
Fitzgerald, William: CURE FOR A YLITH   Short story.
     What better way to strike at a well-guarded tyrant
than through his own innermost fears of treachery and deceit
and revolt.
Simak, Clifford D: LIMITING FACTOR   Short story.
     Explorers from Earth discover a planet-sized computer
that was apparently abandoned by its original owners and
builders because it was--obsolete.
Lafayette, Rene: THE EMPEROR OF THE UNIVERSE Short story.
     Interesting story about the crazy old spaceman who
turned out to be the Johnny Appleseed of the future, making
the Universe safe for the humans who followed him from world
to world and from star to star. Sixth in the Conquest of
Space series.
Cover artist: Earle Bergey (The Other World)
Editor: Sam Merwin, Jr.

JANUARY, 1950   VOL. 20. NO. 3.
Hamilton, Edmond: THE RETURN OF CAPTAIN FUTURE Novelette.
     First in a series of novelettes featuring the further
exploits of Curt Newton and the Futuremen, probably better
written but not quite as much fun as the original novels.
In this one the Futuremen return from another galaxy, bear-
ing with them a living survivor of the Linid, the non-human
race that once ruled the Universe before the rise of mankind
and its contemporaries.
Kent, Kelvin: ROMAN HOLIDAY   Novelette.
     First of the marvelously funny and imaginative Pete

65

Manx time-travel stories written by Henry Kuttner under one of his many pseudonyms, reprinted from Thrilling Wonder Stories, August, 1939. In this one Pete plays havoc with the Roman Empire and one of his associates proves that Caesar's wife is truly above reproach.

Morrison, William: STARS OVER SANTA CLAUS   Short story.
How do you celebrate Christmas properly a hundred light years in space when your materializer is not functioning up to par?

Lafayette, Rene: THE LAST ADMIRAL   Short story.
Last of the Conquest of Space series, telling how old Admiral Barnell proved everyone was wrong who said that he and the Space Navy were outmoded and useless.

St. Clair, Margaret: HATHOR'S PETS   Short story.
When a superior alien makes pets of humans, they would be wise to bow to the inevitable and not push their luck, else their predicament might become even worse--

Groves, J. W: REGROWTH   Short story.
Will the real Doctor Walker please step forward?

MacDonald, John D: THE FIRST ONE   Short story.
The first man into space was supposed to be a fake, but Bus Bannister had other ideas about that--

Cover artist: Earle Bergey (The Return of Captain Future)
Editor: Sam Merwin, Jr.

MARCH, 1950   VOL. 21. NO. 1.
Hawkins, Ward: MEN MUST DIE   Novelette.
Reprinted from Thrilling Wonder Stories, April, 1939, this Hall of Fame classic tells how a courageous Earthman used trickery to save his race and that of the Jovians from the dread scourge of the Lubian invaders. Not too bad for its time.

Jones, Raymond F: ENCROACHMENT   Novelette.
How to use the eons of past Earthly time to save an alien race that seemingly has no future. Interesting philosophical concepts in this one, from a past master of brain-teasers such as Renaissance and The Alien.

Powell, Ted: THE SIGN AND THE MESSAGE   Short story.
This one is almost too cute for its own good, as you will understand when you read the final paragraph.

Lee, Matt: APPOINTMENT IN NEW UTRECHT   Short story.
Another time-travel story about the inevitability of a man's Fate, whatever it may be.

Cover artist: Earle Bergey (The Lady Is a Witch)
Editor: Sam Merwin, Jr.

MAY, 1950   VOL. 21. NO. 2.
Hamilton, Edmond: CHILDREN OF THE SUN   ' Novelette.

The Futuremen attempt to save their friend, Philip
Carlin, guest hero of Red Sun of Danger, from a strange and
poetic destiny within the heart of fiery Vulcan.
Kummer, Jr., Frederic Arnold: SIGNBOARD OF SPACE Novelette.
    Superior interplanetary, first published in Thrilling
Wonder Stories, December, 1939, telling of the true meaning
of the canals of Mars, and of the deadly virus that causes
complete petrification of all living flesh.
Leiber, Jr., Fritz: THE BLACK EWE   Short story.
    Nice little chiller about the unlucky Lavinia Simes
and her affect on history.
De Camp, L. Sprague: SUMMER WEAR   Short story.
    Ironic little item about drastic and sudden changes—
relatively speaking—in interstellar fashions.
Jacobi, Carl: THE HISTORIAN   Short story.
    Cute short short about somebody who literally took
science fiction magazines too seriously.
Cover artist: Earle Bergey (Wine of the Dreamers)
Editor: Sam Merwin, Jr.

JULY, 1950   VOL. 21. NO. 3.
Brackett, Leigh: THE TRUANTS   Novelette.
    A completely different kind of story from what is
usually associated with this talented author of vigorous and
two-fisted space opera epics, one more in accord with the
feminine side of her nature. Poignant, poetic and pathetic,
this is the story of super-powerful aliens terrorizing our
civilization who turn out to be just lonely kids on the run
from their own, far-off world.
Smith, Dr. Edward E: ROBOT NEMESIS   Novelette.
    Hall of Fame classic reprinted from Thrilling Wonder
Stories, June, 1939, that was originally part of the famous
round-robin serial, Cosmos, to which many famed authors of
the genre contributed. This segment tells how Ferdinand
Stone outwitted and destroyed those survivors of the robot
hordes that had managed to escape dissolution by the sonic
vibrations of Narodny, the eccentric Russian genius, in "The
Last Poet and the Robots."
Vance, Jack: THE SPA OF THE STARS   Short story.
    Magnus Ridolph searches for a way to save Joe Blaine's
interplanetary resort hotel from economic and physical disaster.
Bradbury, Ray: PURPOSE   Short story.
    A deserted alien city waits twenty thousand years to
fulfill its purpose—
Sheldon, Walt: MUSIC OF THE SPHERES   Short story.
    The greatest terrors in space may well come from
within a man rather than from without.

Long, Frank Belknap: INVASION   Short story.
     For once, the Martians are not the nasties in this
one. An invasion of kindness--
Morrison, William: DISAPPOINTMENT   Short story.
     Horton Perry, the salted nut king, is a hard man to
please, as you are sure to agree after reading this mildly
amusing little story of his son-in-law's successes and
failures.
Cover artist: Earle Bergey (The City At World's End)
Editor: Sam Merwin, Jr.

SEPTEMBER, 1950   VOL. 22. NO. 1.
Hamilton, Edmond: THE HARPERS OF TITAN   Novelette.
     Excellent Captain Future story of the people of
Saturn's largest moon and the strange cult of the Harpers
that obsessed them almost to madness, and of how Simon
Wright, the bodiless brain and long-time mentor of Curt Newton, had to take on full human guise once more in order to
combat this bizarre menace.
Barnes, Arthur K. & Kuttner, Henry: THE ENERGY EATERS
     Anthony Quade and Gerry Carlyle   Novelette.
join forces in an uneasy alliance of friendly enemies in order to save Hollywood on the Moon from a bizarre invasion of
tribble-like creatures that soak up all the energy in sight
and reproduce like mad. Reprinted from Thrilling Wonder
Stories, Oct., 1939.
Vance, Jack: COSMIC HOTFOOT   Short story.
     Magnus Ridolph plumbs the mystery of the inexplicable
disappearances on the eccentric world of Jexjeka.
Reynolds, Mack: DOWN THE RIVER   Short story.
     Ironic little story of how human racial prejudices are
dumped right back on our heads when Earth becomes a pawn in
a game of interstellar politics.
Lee, Matt: EXIT LINE   Short story.
     Unusual little classic that is a great rarity in
science fiction--a humorous BEM story. It tells of the wily
and amiable lorum and how it conned the gullible colonists
from Earth into--but read the story for yourself.
Cover artist: Earle Bergey (The Cybernetic Brains)
Editor: Sam Merwin, Jr.

NOVEMBER, 1950   VOL. 22. NO. 2.
Hamilton, Edmond: PARDON MY IRON NERVES   Novelette.
     Amusing story of Captain Future's robot pal, Grag, and
the nervous breakdown he imagined he was about to suffer,
caused from being in intimate contact with humans so much of
the time. How he quells the revolt of the "free" mining
machines on Dis, remote satellite of Pluto, is a riot.

Hubbard, L. Ron: TOUGH OLD MAN   Novelette.
     Fairly competently written story with a plot that is
so old that it has moss on it a foot thick: the western
transferred to interplanetary space, or the saga of the
green young recruit determined to make good under the
tutelage of the toughest old lawman in the universe, condemned to serving in the worst hell-hole of outer space.
Really sounds familiar, doesn't it?
Phillips, Rog: LOVE MY ROBOT   Short story.
     Story of robot behavior specialist, Ken Renard, and
the super-robot that he must uncover from amongst a thousand
others; this situation really pre-figures the very similar
ones in Philip K. Dick's novel of androids in hiding and the
dystopian movie that followed it by several decades.
Williams, Robert Moore: ROAD BLOCK   Short story.
     Neat little item of an inborn weakness in the human
brain that prevents it ever from being used as a mechanism
for mentally controlled creation, and man's determination to
detour around this cosmic road block.
Reynolds, Mack: TALL TALE   Short story.
     Another time travel story about modern schmos acciden-
tally transported backwards into the past. This time two
jet pilots visit the good old days of Jim Bridger, mountain
man.
Cover artist: Earle Bergey (The Five Gold Bands)
Editor: Sam Merwin, Jr.

     Note: Starting with this issue there were no more
Hall of Fame reprint stories from old Wonder Stories, Wonder
Quarterly, or Thrilling Wonder. Fantastic Story Magazine
had been brought into being for that precise purpose, and
all reprint material was confined to that publication from
then on. "The Energy Eaters" collaboration by Arthur K.
Barnes and Henry Kuttner in the preceding issue was, there-
fore, the final reprint to grace the pages of Startling
Stories, except for two or three novels already mentioned in
the section on novels that had seen previous book publication only a few years earlier.

JANUARY, 1951   VOL. 22. NO. 3.
Liddell, C. H: THE ODYSSEY OF YIGGAR THROLG   Novelette.
     Amusing, Unknown-type novelette of the various misad-
ventures of a much-beleaguered gnome out of Norse mythology,
thrust out into the world of modern men to search for an
answer to the dread curse of cold iron that separates him
from his intended bride. Really pure fantasy rather than
science fiction, and written, if I am not much mistaken, by
Henry Kuttner under one of his pseudonyms.

Hamilton, Edmond: MOON OF THE UNFORGOTTEN   Novelette.
     Another well-written entry in this series of shorter
pieces in the long-enduring saga of Curt Newton and the
Futuremen, wherein the intrepid quartet attempt to utilize a
long-forgotten secret of ancient Europan science to unlock
the secret to humanity's ultimate origins that lie hidden
within the human brain itself.
Sprague, Carter: TIME TRACK   Short story.
     Interesting story of time-travel along parallel paths
of human development and -- imminent world catastrophe.
Sheldon, Walt: REPLICA   Short story.
     Another parallel time-travel story, not quite as
serious as the preceding, wherein the process is used to
help reinforce the credibility of two-bit wild west movies.
Osborne, Robertson: CRITERION   Short story.
     Another good story with a trick ending, such as were
so popular with the E.C. science fiction horror comics of
the fifties, but lacking the gruesomeness, wherein both
humans and aliens alike learn the folly of jumping to con-
clusions and judging solely by outward appearances.
Cover artist: Earle Bergey (Passport to Jupiter)
Editor: Sam Merwin, Jr.

MARCH, 1951   VOL. 23. NO. 1.
Hamilton, Edmond: EARTHMEN NO MORE   Novelette.
     Probably the most serious in tone of all the Captain
Future stories, either the early novels or the later
novelettes, concerning a man of the late twentieth century
revived from a deep freeze in space to face the mind-
boggling marvels--and difficulties--of the far future.
Well-written and thought provoking.
Temple, William F: THE TWO SHADOWS   Novelette.
     Hard-boiled, realistic story of the last three sur-
vivors on Mars of the nuclear holocaust that destroyed Earth
and most of the human race, and how their personal problems
were eventually resolved. Well-drawn characters, the very
antithesis of the space opera archetypes, but none for whom
I could find much sympathy.
St. Clair, Margaret: THEN FLY OUR GREETINGS Short story.
     Chilling story of a government project to develop a
new super-weapon that succeeded beyond its wildest dreams.
Vance, Jack: MEN OF THE TEN BOOKS   Short story.
     The people of a long-lost Earth colony entertain
vastly exaggerated ideals of cultural and scientific perfec-
tion, and do their very best to live up to them.
Merwin, Jr., Sam: SHORT ORDER   Short story.
     Another story with a trick ending, with its predict-
able punchline in the last two or three paragraphs.

Cover artist: Earle Bergey (The Starmen of Llyrdis--symbolic presentation)
Editor: Sam Merwin, Jr.

MAY, 1951   VOL. 23. NO. 2.
Lee, Matt: LETTERS OF FIRE   Novelette.
     Longish novelette about the impact of interstellar civilization upon terrestrial culture, particularly the Hollywood movie industry--and vice versa.
Hamilton, Edmond: BIRTHPLACE OF CREATION   Novelette.
     Last of the Captain Future series, more or less of a sequel to the earlier novel, The Quest Beyond the Stars (Captain Future, Winter, 1942), wherein the Futuremen first discovered the wondrous Birthplace from whence all matter in our universe comes into being, and to which they now return to keep a power-hungry madman from subjecting it to his destructive whims.   Better written than the earlier novel, but not nearly as much fun.
Wyndham, John: AND THE WALLS CAME TUMBLING DOWN
     Enjoyable story of an alien   Short story.
expedition to Earth by silicon beings who completely misunderstand the nature of the inhabitants and their strange, devastating--weapons?   Written by a real old-timer from the early years of Wonder Stories, who then wrote under the name of John Beynon or John Beynon Harris.
Williams, Robert Moore: TAME ME THIS BEAST   Short story.
     Professor Shaler learned too late that you cannot fool around with the inner nature of man with impunity, modern or savage.
Mines, Samuel: A TAXABLE DIMENSION   Short story.
     Mildly amusing story of how perfect counterfeiting might be accomplished by utilizing another dimension of space.
Cover artist: Earle Bergey (The Seed From Space--symbolic presentation)
Editor: Sam Merwin, Jr.

JULY, 1951   VOL. 23. NO. 3
Brackett, Leigh: THE WOMAN FROM ALTAIR   Novelette.
     Engrossing story of merciless revenge from beyond the stars, by the mistress of rip-roaring space operas in the old-fashioned tradition.   This novelette is something of a departure from her usual style but very well-handled.   With a few changes in locale, situation and general environment, it could almost have passed muster as one of those revenge horror stories that were so popular in the Weird Tales of the twenties and thirties.   Too bad Ahrian never went up against Jules de Grandin.

71

Sprague, Carter: THE ULTIMATE ENGINE   Short story.
    Neat little item which states that physical perfection
certainly isn't everything, particularly when your mind may
very well prove to be the means of your personal salvation.
Matheson, Richard: WITCH WAR   Short story.
    Another Unknown-type story, this time of teen-aged
witches waging warfare with psychic--or psi?--powers.
Cover artist: Earle Bergey (The Dark Tower)
Editor: Sam Merwin, Jr.

SEPTEMBER, 1951   VOL. 24. NO. 1.
Gault, William Campbell: THIS WAY TO MARS   Novelette.
    Account of a future civilization wherein women are now
the dominant sex, and the down-trodden males are planning a
revolt to regain their rights.
Vance, Jack: THE MASQUERADE ON DICANTROPUS   Short story.
    Story of interstellar misdirection by a master of the
genre.
Fyfe, H. B: YES, SIR!   Short story.
    Robot story, of an automaton with a very limited pur-
pose and function.
MacDonald, John D: THE WHITE FRUIT OF BANALDAR
    Another short goodie by the   Short story.
hard-boiled master of suspense, this one an interplanetary
tale of returning to nature with a vengeance, on the decep-
tively idyllic world of Banaldar.
Samalman, Alexander: THE LAST STORY   Short story.
    Very neat little short story about a future in which
literature of all kinds is strictly prohibited, and of the
last author and the last editor who broke that law.
Cover artist: Earle Bergey (House of Many Worlds)
Editor: Samuel Mines

NOVEMBER, 1951   VOL. 24. NO. 2.
Reynolds, Mack & Brown, Fredric: THE GAMBLERS   Novelette.
    Excellent story of a spaceman on the Moon playing a
bizarre kind of Russian roulette with aliens bent on the
Earth's conquest, the fate of his world the stakes. More
serious theme than usual with this pair, who usually collaborated for stories of a much lighter bent.
Merwin, Jr., Sam: GREASE IN THE PAN   Short story.
    Still another trick ending story, this one about an
alien contactee who made a fatal error about what was really
the dominant life-form on Earth.
Morrison, William: THE CUPIDS OF VENUS   Short story.
    Entertaining but a bit-too-cute story of the subtle
and devious matchmakers who set up the future colonists of
Venus--in more ways than one.

Cover artist: Alex Schomburg (The Star Watchers)
Editor: Samuel Mines

JANUARY, 1952   VOL. 24. NO. 3.
Chandler, A. Bertram: LOST ART   Novelette.
     By the author of the long-running Commodore Grimes
series, a story about a lost interstellar art form, and the
two greedy men who wished it revived, for a price, of
course.
Gallun, Raymond Z: THE GREAT IDEA   Short story.
     A great idea for making Earth-to-Moon travel cheaper
and easier that really wasn't so great.
Wyndham, John: THE WHEEL   Short story.
     Neat little anti-technology, post-catastrophe short
short.
Reynolds, Mack: HOW GREEN WAS MY MARTIAN   Short story.
     Wildly funny little story about a hilarious breakdown
in interplanetary communication.
Cover artist: Earle Bergey (Journey to Barkut)
Editor: Samuel Mines

FEBRUARY, 1952   VOL. 25. NO 1.
Pratt, Fletcher: A VIOLATION OF RULES   Novelette.
     More mental gymnastics from a grand old master of the
genre. Time travel paradoxes galore in this one, with
shunting of minds back and forth from one era to another,
despite violations of the fundamental laws of the universe.
Oliver, Chad: THE SUBVERSIVES   Short story.
     Another story with a trick ending that would have not
been out of place in the old E.C. science fiction horror
comics, Weird Fantasy or Weird Science, treating this time
with interplanetary spies on a quiz show.
Brackett, Leigh: THE SHADOWS   Short story.
     Another different style of story for this very fine
author, wherein it is proved that it really pays to know who
your friends and enemies are, particularly on a new and
unexplored world.
Henderson, Gene L: THE LAST SPACEMAN   Short story.
     Story of the first man into space, and why he should
never have come back alive.
Doar, Graham: WHO KNOWS HIS BROTHER   Short story.
     Ironic and tragic tale of the bitter and unceasing
warfare waged by the mutant successors of man upon one
another because of their fundamental misconception of what
constitutes true humanity.
Cover artist: Earle Bergey (Vulcan's Dolls)
Editor: Samuel Mines

MARCH, 1952   VOL. 25. NO. 2.
Crossen, Kendell Foster: THINGS OF DISTINCTION   Novelette.
        Amusing story of future interstellar big business,
mainly concerning attempts to sell headgear to intelligent
insects with their own, built-in halos.
Oliver, Chad: LADY KILLER   Short story.
        Looking for mates on Mars because all Earth females
are now sterile from radiation, but the Martians are not
quite what's expected--
Sheldon, Walt: THE HUNTERS   Short story.
        Neat trick ending short short, but predictable.
Cover artist: Earle Bergey (The Well of the Worlds)
Editor: Samuel Mines

APRIL, 1952   VOL. 25. NO. 3.
Brackett, Leigh, THE LAST DAYS OF SHANDAKOR   Novelette.
        Much more in Brackett's usual style is this long
novelette about the great old lost race of Mars and the
modern Earthman who caught a glimpse of them in their prime
in the enchanted streets of old Shandakor.   Excellent combination of space opera and the lost race genre, always this
author's peculiar specialty.
Saari, Oliver: THE INTRUDER   Short story.
        Another of those maddening little stories about an ex-
act duplicate in all respects taking the place of the
protagonist--and he can do nothing to stop it!
Fritch, Charles E: WELCOME TO LUNA   Short story.
        Ironic short short about the man who was determined to
be the first man on the Moon, despite cynicism and opposition from family and friends.
Herbert, Frank: LOOKING FOR SOMETHING?   Short story.
        Early short by this very famous modern author, typi-
cally provocative in style, about inter-galactic watchers
fearful that humanity might somehow learn to see the cosmos
as it really is and not as they imagine it to be--???
Cover artist: Alex Schomburg (Welcome to Luna)
Editor: Samuel Mines

MAY, 1952   VOL. 26. NO. 1.
Crossen, Kendell Foster: THE GNOME'S GNEISS   Novelette.
        Another Unknownish-type fantasy rather than science
fiction, this one about a modern man looking for work who
embarks on a weird odyssey into the realm of the Norse Gods
to save the world from impending Ragnarok.
St. Clair, Margaret: THE MURALIST   Short story.
        How an ancient reptilian civilization was brought to
its downfall by the lowly proto-mice of Earth, leaving no
one in later ages to understand the historical mural of

Vesta.

Russell, Eric Frank: TAKE A SEAT   Short story.
     Ironic little story about an alien invader who got
into the wrong body, that of a condemned murderer about to
undergo sentences of electrocution.

Zocks, Robert: FROM OUTER SPACE   Short story.
     Doomsday comes, of sorts, when offended aliens of por-
cine ancestry put Earth off limits to the rest of the
galaxy—and vice versa!

Cover artist: Alex Schomburg (The Hellflower)
Editor: Samuel Mines

JUNE, 1952   VOL. 26. NO. 2.

Vance, Jack: SABOTAGE ON SULFUR PLANET   Novelette.
     Good adult space opera about Robert Smith's search for
an unknown planet of sentient creatures being rapidly exter-
minated by utterly ruthless human buccaneers of space for
the sake of jewels as natural to them as pearls are to an
oyster.

Fritch, Charles E: THE WATCHER   Short story.
     Bradbury-like story of the strange castaway who
patiently awaited the coming of more human expeditions to
Mars, and more and more—

Roman, Tarr: SKIN DEEP   Short story.
     Cute story about a smart Earthman who thought he could
make a killing selling cosmetics to reptilian aliens,
without first ascertaining what they really used the stuff
for.

Townes, Robert Sherman: PROBLEM FOR EMMY   Short story.
     Probably one of the first adult computer stories, of
its pathetic attempts to attain some measure of self-
identification.

Boucher, Anthony: THE AMBASSADORS   Short story.
     As much fantasy as science fiction, this amusing
little short short is about werewolves being selected as the
first ambassadors to the canine-descended inhabitants of
Mars.

McGregor, R. J: Short story.
     Bitter little story about just how there came to be
more than one moon in the night skies of Earth, thanks to
human duplicity, greed and falsehood.

Cover artist: Earle Bergey (Dragon's Island)
Editor: Samuel Mines

JULY, 1952   VOL. 26. NO. 3.

Jones, Raymond F: COLLISION   Novelette.
     Story of love and survival in outer space after a
spaceship rams space station. Adult, well-written tale, but

a little talky and dull.

Clarke, Arthur C: ALL THE TIME IN THE WORLD   Short story.
     Different kind of time-travel story, what one might expect from this fine author.

Morrison, William: NEW UNIVERSE   Short story.
     Zeron, lord of this universe, ventures into new dimensions, seeking new universes to conquer, without reckoning the price he might have to pay, which is a stiff one--

Smith, Phyllis Sterling: THE BEST POLICY   Short story.
     Amusing story of Martian visitors to this world scarcely able to understand the concept of falsehood as practiced by the natives, so foreign is it to their own natures.

DeFord, Miriam Allen: MR. CIRCE   Short story.
     Fantasy story of a man with an unusual talent that tended to get out of hand. The title really tells it all.

Rocklynne, Ross: COURTESY CALL   Short story.
     Little did the visitor from Pundar realize he was undergoing a severe test upon which might rest the future of his world--and Earth's--

Cover artist: Alex Schomburg (Passport to Pax)
Editor: Samuel Mines

AUGUST, 1952   VOL. 27. NO. 1.

Crossen, Kendell Foster: THE HOUR OF THE MORTALS Novelette.
     Mortal humanity turns in outrage upon its immortal clique of privileged rulers, until diplomat Fenimore redresses the balance of power and sanity.

Neal, Harry: PAGE AND PLAYER   Novelette.
     The violent Earthmen were contemptuous of the peaceful Cronies, but they did seem to have a way of getting things done--

Fritch, Charles E: MAJOR VENTURE AND THE MISSING SATELLITE
     Lighthearted spoof of the   Short story.
Captain Future interplanetary epics, but just a little too cute for my personal taste.

Ellanby, Boyd: FAMILY TREE   Short story.
     Scientists attempting to tamper with the past unwittingly arouse the ire of forces that now threaten their own time with destruction.

Vance, Jack: NOISE   Short story.
     Story of a castaway in space who heard strange noises--real or imaginary?

Dryfoos, Dave: HERE LIES BOTTLETHWAITE   Short story.
     Cute story of an alien intelligence that proves its existence by cheating to attain its ends.

Cover artist: Earle Bergey (The Lovers)
Editor: Samuel Mines

SEPTEMBER, 1952   VOL. 27. NO. 2.
Dee, Roger: THE OBLIGATION   Novelette.
     Excellent story of an alien being's sense of obliga-
tion to the human who had rendered it a valuable service,
with a real kicker in the last few words of the final sen-
tence.
McGregor, R. J: THE PERFECT GENTLEMAN   Short story.
     Earthgirl marooned on a distant planet envisions her
ideal of a perfect gentleman, but she never really expected
him to materialize into reality--
Fritch, Charles E: NIGHT TALK   Short story.
     Short short about the--concidental?--duplication of a
certain blessed event, this time on poor, old, polluted,
used-up Mars--
Cover artist: Walter Popp (Big Planet)
Editor: Samuel Mines

OCTOBER, 1952   VOL. 27. NO. 3.
De Camp, L. Sprague: THE GUIDED MAN   Novelette.
     By the old master of irony, satirical, and generally
amusing science fiction, a short epic of the Telegog Company
and the unique new service it offered its customers, long-
distance mental guidance and coaching by remote control.
Interesting concept.
DeFord, Miriam Allen: THE THROWBACK   Short story.
     In the perfectly ordered world of the thirtieth cen-
tury, a normal mother is considered an atavistic freak.
Quietly chilling story in the tradition of Brave New World.
Smith, Phyllis Sterling: NOTICE OF INTENT   Short story.
     From Mars comes the wonder drug to end all wonder
drugs--Marcillin--and a selfish plot by Earthly monopolists
to corner the market on this precious new commodity.
Miller, Jr., Walter: GRAVESONG   Short story.
     By the author of A Canticle For Leibowitz, an early
story of the two divergent paths of evolution humanity took,
to the stars and to the--
Whiteside, Stanley: DISPOSAL   Short story.
     Story of a sort of Venusian Galloway Gallagher, a
drunken genius who invents unusual gadgets for which at
first there appears to be no useful purpose.
Cover artist: Jack Coggins (Four Centuries of Planets? --
article)
Editor: Samuel Mines

NOVEMBER, 1952   VOL. 28. NO. 1.
McGregor, R. J: THE CROOK IN TIME   Novelette.
     Bizarre story of time travel and future crime. Really
hard to analyze in a few words. A little too outlandishly

77

oddball to be really funny.

Rogers, Joel Townsley: THE NIGHT THE WORLD TURNED OVER
    Old-fashioned world-catastrophe   Novelette.
story wherein the title pretty much tells it like it is--

De Camp, L. Sprague: PROPOSAL   Short story.
    Another outrageously amusing interplanetary yarn by
the old master of science fiction comedy, this one about a
scaly alien with a yen for a pretty Earthgirl.

Dryfoos, Dave: SOME LIKE IT COLD   Short story.
    Interstellar aliens mistakenly judge Earthly behavior
by their own standards.

Cover artist: Walter Popp (The Star Dice)
Editor: Samuel Mines

DECEMBER, 1952   VOL. 28. NO. 2.

Merril, Judith: WHOEVER YOU ARE   Novelette.
    Love story about an Earth starship that returned from
its voyage with a load of alien visitors, and the effect
they wrought upon the suspicious terrestrials who received
their overtures of peace and friendship with mixed feelings.

Crossen, Kendell Foster: LOVE THAT AIR   Novelette.
    Another satiric epic of interstellar big business and
flamboyant salesmanship, this time selling flavored wood
candy to super-civilized beavers.

DeFord, Miriam Allen: THE CHILDREN   Novelette.
    Interesting story of the time-traveler, McElroy, and
his various descendants that he encountered throughout the
ages.

Farmer, Philip Jose: SAIL ON! SAIL ON!   Short story.
    Alternate world story of Columbus' momentous voyage,
and how it might have ended had the conditions been right.

West, H. H: THE BOOK OF THE DEAD   Short short.
    Post-catastrophe short short of a would-be world dic-
tator, and the ironic aftermath of the holocaust that he
deliberately sowed--

Dickson, Gordon R: SHOW ME THE WAY TO GO HOME   Short story.
    Amusing little story of two alien observers on Earth--
and their talking cat!

Cover artist: Emsh (The Long View)
Editor: Samuel Mines

JANUARY, 1953   VOL. 28. NO. 3.

Leinster, Murray: OVERDRIVE   Novelette.
    Well-written, old-fashioned space opera by an old
master of this type of literature, concerning a member of
the profession whose business it was to prevent warfare between planets, and the imbroglio he encountered in interstellar space, complete with space pirates, aliens and

mutiny.

Gunn, James E: THE BOY WITH FIVE FINGERS   Short story.
     Three-pager about a post-catastrophe civilization of
therimorphic mutants, and the five-fingered boy who was a
throwback to the Old Race.

Crossen, Kendell Foster: MY OLD VENUSIAN HOME   Short story.
     Take off on Uncle Tom's Cabin, southern hospitality,
and the plantation system of the Deep South, set on Venus,
with an overly officious saurian cast as the Venusian Uncle
Tom.

Dee, Roger: NO CHARGE TO THE MEMBERSHIP   Short story.
     Slightly satirical story of an editor of a fanzine
called--Cosmicrud!?--who is visited by real aliens from
outer space, and what results from that unexpected meeting.

Asimov, Isaac: BUTTON, BUTTON   Short story.
     One of the Robotics Master's infrequent appearances in
the pages of Startling Stories, this time with a cute little
story about an eccentric old man's device for transmitting
valuable documents from the past, and the simple but basic
flaw in his scheme that made it fail.

Lewis, Jack: WHO'S CRIBBING?   Short story.
     See if you can figure out just who is copying who in
this one.

Vance, Jack: THREE-LEGGED JOE   Short story.
     Meet Three-legged Joe, Oldfar's Old Man of the Sea of
space--
Cover artist: Alex Schomburg (Overdrive)
Editor: Samuel Mines

FEBRUARY, 1953   VOL. 29. NO. 1.
Pratt, Fletcher: POTEMKIN VILLAGE   Novelette.
     Model village in an experimental colony on Venus where
something seems to be wrong--
Asimov, Isaac: THE MONKEY'S FINGERS   Short story.
     Combine cybernetics with a typewriting monkey, and
you've got troubles.
Knight, Damon: DEFINITION   Short story.
     Charles Samson solves the centuries-old riddle of the
galaxy-hopping Kassids, much to mankind's dismay.
Cover artist: Emsh (Potemkin Village)
Editor: Samuel Mines

MARCH, 1953   VOL. 29. NO. 2.
Oliver, Chad: THE SHORE OF TOMORROW   Novelette.
     War between Earth and Titan, with an alien spy on
board the first spaceship to reach Saturn's largest satellite, a spy who thought he was human--
Slotkin, Joseph: THE GINGERBREAD HOUSE   Short story.

Oddball little fantasy about how Hansel and Gretel grew up, and what happened to them after the fairy tale as loyal members of the Communist Party of the Eastern Zone.

Bretnor, R: THE SOUL OF THE OISUTA   Short story.

Another fantasy, this one about how to persuade oysters to grow gems instead of pearls, except that oysters are not the same the world over.

Jameson Sr. & Jr., Colin G: OUTSIGHT   Short story.

Engrossing story of a girl's premonition of her father's bizarre and unexpected return from the stars.

Ksanda, Charles F: STEPPING STONE   Short story.

Bradbury-like story of the strange interstellar dreamer who lay in wait on Mars for the unsuspecting explorers from Earth and whose dreams he made real.

Shay, Harry J: THE AMBASSADOR FROM THE 21ST CENTURY

Short short about a visitor   Short story.
from nowhere with a disturbing message of doom.

Cover artist: Walter Popp (   )
Editor: Samuel Mines

APRIL, 1953   VOL. 29. NO. 3.

Rocklynne, Ross: FULFILLMENT   Novelette.

Interesting story of an alien race that passes judgment on mankind for their emotional and psychological shortcomings, and forbids them the conquest of space until they are worthy of it--and the stubborn human who tried to prove they were wrong.

Townes, Robert Sherman: EARTH IS THE EVENING STAR

Another passable Bradbury   Short story.
imitation, about the first Earthmen on Mars and how they solved the mystery of the strange immortal city with no inhabitants.

Locke, Robert Donald: THRESHOLD   Short story.

Far future story of a rigidly regulated Terran society, and the iconoclastic brother from the wild Centaurian frontier whose radical ideas threw a monkey wrench into the gears of civilization.

Merwin, Jr., Sam: DISTORTION PATTERN   Short story.

Science fantasy about godlike creatures from outer space who, just for the Hell of it, meddle in the mundane love affairs of terrestrial mortals.

Bigelow, Leslie: CLOCKWORK   Short story.

Superior mad scientist story, about a master of clockwork mechanisms and fourth dimensional mathematics who plans to remake the world to his design.

Phillips, Peter: LILA   Short story.

Interplanetary newscaster, Buzz Boothby, is haunted by a mysterious girl who disrupts his life and eventually com-

pletely changes it—for the better?
Barr, Richard & West, Wallace: RUBBERNECK   Short story.
    Cute short short about just what really is the reason
behind the visits of all these flying saucers to our little
planet.
Cover artist: Emsh (Halos, Inc.)
Editor: Samuel Mines

MAY, 1953   VOL. 30. NO. 1.
Loomis, Noel: WE BREATHE FOR YOU   Novelette.
    By the old-time author of City of Glass and Iron Men,
an intriguing story of a future technology that promises to
do almost everything for its customers, but has it con-
tracted for more than it can handle when it offers to—??
Bigelow, Leslie: THE IMMOVABLE OBJECT   Short story.
    Imaginative story of outer space aliens who used Earth
for an inadvertent dumping ground millennia ago without
humanity being aware of it—until now!
Shallit, Joseph: MATING TIME   Short story.
    Familiar retelling of the Adam and Eve story, with
educated bugs mating two humans on a distant planet to start
a new race.
Dickson, Gordon R: THE THREE   Short story.
    Interesting story by the famed author of the Dorsai
stories about a weird symbiosis between man, a woman and an
alien plant.
Cover artist: Walter Popp (The Conditioned Captain)
Editor: Samuel Mines

JUNE, 1953   VOL. 30. NO. 2.
Holden, Fox B: HERE LIE WE   Novelette.
    Excellent adult science fiction—the first expedition
to Mars from Earth discover the Martians on the verge of total racial extinction because their share of the universal
life force has finally run out. Intriguing concept, and
very well-written without being maudlin and soap-operish.
Waltham, Leslie: IMPERFECTION   Short story.
    Another story wherein robots are trying to masquerade
as flesh-and-blood humans, even to the extent of marrying
into their ranks.
Young, Robert F: THE BLACK DEEP THOU WINGEST Short story.
    By the master of sentimental science fiction. A man
has disturbing memories on a forgotten, backwater planet on
the perimeter of Galactic civilization.
Cover artist: Emsh (The Black Deep Thou Wingest)
Editor: Samuel Mines

AUGUST, 1953   VOL. 30. NO. 3.

Sturgeon, Theodore: THE WAGES OF SYNERGY   Novelette.
          Science fiction murder mystery about a scientist who
has discovered a perfect method of causing undetectable mur-
ders chemically, and how he utilizes it for the benefit of a
man mad for power. As usual with Sturgeon, well-written,
adult and engrossing.
Sloan, Ralph: THE RUNAWAY TRICYCLE   Short story.
          Psychological tale, of regression under stress in
outer space.
Ratigan, William: NEVER TEMPT THE DEVIL   Short story.
          Fantasy about a man who read about tomorrow's news in
today's paper. Familiar.
Smith, George H: THE LAST SPRING   Short story.
          Refugees from Earth find their own place in the sun--
literally.
Cover artist: Walter Popp (The Wages of Synergy)
Editor: Samuel Mines

OCTOBER, 1953   VOL. 31. NO. 1.
Clinton, Jr., Ed M: OVERLOAD   Novelette.
          Story of mechanically tapping and recording the
storehouse of knowledge and memories in the human brain, and
of the various men who wanted to use it either for good or
evil.
Hamilton, Edmond: THE UNFORGIVEN   Short story.
          Adult interplanetary fiction about a hero with a
guilt-complex.
McMorrow, Jr., Tom: OUT OF THE WELL   Short story.
          Ironic short short about the possible reincarnation of
a ruthless politician in the wrong sort of body.
Leinster, Murray: THE JEZEBEL   Short story.
          Science fiction comedy, about an eccentric experimen-
ter who attempts to adapt philosophical concepts to practical usages, with sometimes explosive results.
Cover artist: Alex Schomburg (Overload)
Editor: Samuel Mines

JANUARY, 1954   VOL. 31. NO. 2.
Crossen, Kendell Foster: HIS HEAD IN THE CLOUDS Novelette.
          Sort of a Walter Mitty story of the future, with a
dreaming protagonist who has a penchant for attracting all
kinds of bizarre problems.
Shallit, Joseph: ESCAPE   Short story.
          Ironic episode of an Earthman's escape from matrimony
on Venus, only to learn that he has gone from the frying pan
straight into the fire.
Slotkin, Joseph: THE UNPREY SPRAY   Short story.
          Strictly logical short short about the ultimate con-

sequences of a spray that does away with the natural preying instinct of all predators.

Dick, Philip K: A PRESENT FOR PAT   Short story.
     Beware of gifts from Ganymede, especially if they happen to be gods, minor or not.
St. Clair, Margaret: THE MONITOR   Short story.
     Quietly chilling story of the Methwyn, the beings who look after the Earthlings whether they want it or not.
Cover artist: Walter Popp (The Time Masters)
Editor: Samuel Mines

SPRING, 1954   VOL. 31. NO. 3.
Brackett, Leigh: RUNAWAY   Novelette.
     Adult, psychological story of a man on the run from himself in an over-complex society of the future. Something of a departure for the two-fisted mistress of space opera, but she handles the theme well, as usual.
Merril, Judith: PEEPING TOM   Novelette.
     Superior story of an inadvertent gift of telepathy to a perfectly ordinary young man, and how he handles it—or is handled by it.
Stearns, Charles A: LITTLE ENOS   Short story.
     Sometimes there can be worse things than ignorance in this world, as a harassed father discovers on Venus in a special kind of school for exceptional children.
Young, Robert F: STOP-OVER   Short story.
     Different reactions of two over-civilized Earthlings of the future to an unspoiled primitive Earth-type planet, one romantic and sentimental, the other intensely practical and selfish.
Peacock, Wilbur S: THE SOUND OF WILLOW PIPES   Short story.
     Post-catastrophe story of what hope still remained for humanity in a war-ravaged world.
Cover artist: Alex Schomburg (The Sound of Willow Pipes)
Editor: Samuel Mines

SUMMER, 1954   VOL. 32. NO. 1.
St. Clair, Margaret: FINDERS KEEPERS   Short story.
     The brow-beaten wife of an asteroid treasure hunter finally gets the last word the hard way—when her mouthy hubby is transformed into something that can't talk back.
Merril, Judith: STORMY WEATHER   Short story.
     Bomb-disposal in outer space by a psi-trained woman with something else on her mind—
Stearns, Charles A: THE GARDEN   Short story.
     A spacewrecked man suddenly realizes that a garden on barren soil is impossible without some kind of organic matter to grow upon, and the only such nearby is another cast-

away spacer.

Merwin, Jr., Sam: SUMMER HEAT   Short story.
        The women of Leithton got really hot when they started
getting pregnant--without cause!
Cover artist: Emsh (The Garden)
Editor: Samuel Mines

FALL, 1954   VOL. 32. NO. 2.
Wallace, F. L: SIMPLE PSIMAN   Novelette.
        Screwball science fiction comedy about telepaths and
teleports in India trying to save Earth from collision with
an errant comet--among other things.
Sambrot, William: GROUNDED   Short story.
        Another Air Force investigation of flying saucers, but
with a bit different kind of results than usual this time.
St. Clair, Margaret: THE MARRIAGE MANUAL   Short story.
        A frustrated human learns from the alien dorff, if you
can't beat the opposite sex then join them.
Cover artist: Alex Schomburg (Grounded)
Editor: Samuel Mines

WINTER, 1955   VOL. 32. NO. 3.
Young, Robert F: MORE STATELY MANSIONS   Novelette.
        Interesting philosophical piece by this always
thoughtful writer of how different people in the next one or
two centuries try to come to terms with what is the true
meaning of happiness.
Marks, Winston: ONLY WITH THINE EYES   Short story.
        Fantasy about a man's hatred for liquor, and what that
resulted in.
Dick, Philip K: HUMAN IS   Short story.
        Unexpected ending and fresh approach to the old
chestnut about aliens from space replacing humans with iden-
tical replicas; for what if the replicas were better than
the originals?
Zacks, Robert: HAVE YOUR PAST READ, MISTER?   Short story.
        Short short fantasy about an unhappy married man who
looked into a crystal ball just to see what might have happened if he hadn't proposed--
Kersh, Thomas: AUDREY'S MOON   Short story.
        About the disadvantages of two telepaths living in
close quarters for too long a time, and the discovery of a
hidden society of telepaths.
Cover artist: Ed Valigursky (Audrey's Moon)
Editor: Samuel Mines

SPRING, 1955   VOL. 33. NO. 1.
Morrison, William: DARK DESTINY   Novelette.

84

Castaways on an alien planet struggle to keep alive the traditions of the Old South, complete with robot darky slaves, until--I'm afraid white supremacists will find the ending of this one a bit hard to take.
Marks, Winston: DOUBLE RATE   Short story.
Telepaths should really do more thinking and less talking, as this story amply proves.
Dick, Philip K: NANNY   Short story.
Survival of the fittest among the robot nursemaids. Imaginative story by this highly original writer.
Dee, Roger: WAYFARER   Short story.
Poignant story of the idiot boy who found acceptance and companionship among the symbiotic alien Wayfarers from the stars.
Matheson, Richard: MISS STARDUST   Short story.
Hilarious little item about the difficulties and tribulations pursuant to holding an interstellar beauty contest, though other writers have handled this sort of story before more effectively.
Porges, Arthur: THE BOX   Short story.
By the master of short, concise, highly original fantasies, a satiric little comment on the competence of the U.S. postal service.
Cover artist: Emsh (Too Late For Eternity)
Editor: Samuel Mines

SUMMER, 1955   VOL. 33. NO. 2.
Young, Robert F: AN APPLE FOR THE TEACHER   Novelette.
How does an ordinary Earth-teacher handle a composition turned in by a pupil who turns out to be an alien from the stars? Simple, when the pupil is smarter than the teacher.
Walton, Bryce: AWAKENING   Novelette.
Another sentimental story about a robot more loving and human than her creators.
Dickson, Gordon R: MOON, JUNE, SPOON, CROON   Short story.
By the co-creator of the Hokas of Toka, a bizarre little item about empathic machines.
Smith, Richard R: THE ANGRY HOUSE   Short story.
How a robot house outsmarted a pair of would-be burglars, without hardly trying.
Coppel, Alfred: TOUCH THE SKY   Short story.
Obviously based on Fortean concepts, this one concerns a man who really did touch the sky.
Waltham, Leslie: THE THIRTEENTH JUROR   Short story.
Interesting story about a future wherein people stand trial for having the wrong emotions rather than for the crimes committed.

DeFord, Miriam Allen: TIME OUT FOR REDHEADS   Short story.
    Average citizen from 2827 takes a vacation in time--
and winds up getting far more than he had bargained for.
Stockheker, R. W: THE ROGUE WAVEFORM   Short story.
    Scientist changes the personality of a villainous
wrestler for the better--maybe.
Cover artist: Emsh (The White Spot)
Editor: Samuel Mines

FAll, 1955   VOL. 33. NO. 3.
Young, Robert F: JUNGLE DOCTOR   Novelette.
    Alien psychiatrist takes a wrong turn somehow and
winds up on a backward planet called--Earth, with somewhat
interesting results for all concerned.
Walton, Bryce: THE GLOB   Short story.
    One man tries to retain his individuality against the
super-consciousness that has engulfed all of humanity.
St. Clair, Margaret: LAZARUS   Short story.
    Nice little shocker about some of the drawbacks in
creating artificial meat.
Reynolds, Mack: COMPLEATED ANGLER   Short story.
    In the regimented world of tomorrow, life in the wild
is hard to find.
O'Hara, Kenneth: SEDIMENT   Short story.
    Mankind is menaced by a creeping evil born out of its
own filth and garbage.
Raines, Theron: HAY FEVER   Short story.
    Short short about a sentient space station with an
allergy--to men.
Marks, Winston: THE SIN   Short story.
    Strange story about a robot corrupted by love, and of
his mistress who could not bear to see him destroyed.
Waltham, Leslie: I LIKE A HAPPY ENDING   Short story.
    Earth dies in seven days, with a whimper, not a bang.
Cover artist: Emsh (The Naked Sky)
Editor: Samuel Mines

    As can readily be seen from a quick glimpse at their
contents, the general quality of shorts and novelettes in
the early years of Startling Stories was not especially
high, except for the reprints from Wonder Stories and
Thrilling Wonder, which were often the best pieces in the
magazine, aside from or even including the featured novel.
After the end of World War II, however, the better writers
were released from service and free to return to their
chosen profession, and the magazine was increased in size
almost by half, affording more space for inclusion of

material other than the lead novel. This change in format
also seemed to coincide with a change in editors, as Oscar
J. Friend left the magazine near the end of 1944 and Sam
Merwin, Jr. took over. I suspect that Friend largely
favored the novel form during his tenure of duty, whereas
Merwin was much more interested in developing and encourag-
ing shorter material of better quality.

In closing, let me say that in its later years, Startling Stories offered shorter pieces of science fiction and
fantasy equal in quality to any similar material being published elsewhere. Entertainment pure and simple was the
primary criterion, and there were fewer message stories and
preachy epics per issue than in comparable issues of John W.
Campbell's Astounding or H. L. Gold's Galaxy. Many of these
stories employed the trick ending of the type utilized so
devastatingly well in the E. C. horror science fiction comics of the fifties, Weird Fantasy and Weird Science, and
these pieces could have been quite easily adapted for inclusion in those publications. Perhaps there were no real
classics of the genre numbered among them, as appeared
within the pages of Astounding, Galaxy, Fantasy and Science
Fiction, and Amazing, or the earlier Wonders, but they were
certainly enjoyable reading most of the time, often thought-
provoking and intellectually stimulating, and that is really
all anyone can expect of any kind of literature.

Appendix I

From Off This World

Edited by Leo Margulies and Oscar J. Friend, and published by Merlin Press in 1949, this volume purports to be a
collection of the best Hall of Fame classic stories
reprinted in the pages of Startling Stories from the earlier
magazines, Science Wonder, Wonder Stories, Wonder Quarterly,
and Thrilling Wonder. On the whole, a pretty fair assort-
ment, except perhaps for Strangland's and Williamson's con-
tributions, which still have their interest as historical
oddities of the genre.

Contents

Gardner, Thomas G: THE LAST WOMAN
Hamilton, Edmond: THE MAN WHO EVOLVED
Herbert, Benson: THE WORLD WITHOUT
Hilliard, A. Rowley: THE GREEN TORTURE
Keller, M.D., David H: THE LITERARY CORKSCREW
Miller, P. Schuyler: THE MAN FROM MARS
Strangland, A. G: THE ANCIENT BRAIN
Smith, Clark Ashton: THE CITY OF THE SINGING FLAME, BEYOND
THE SINGING FLAME
Sharp, D. D: THE ETERNAL MAN
Starzl, R. F: HORNETS OF SPACE
Tucker, Louis D: THE CUBIC CITY
Weinbaum, Stanley G: A MARTIAN ODYSSEY, VALLEY OF DREAMS
Williamson, Jack: THROUGH THE PURPLE CLOUD
Ernst, Paul: THE MICROSCOPIC GIANTS
Kuttner, Henry: WHEN THE EARTH LIVED
Binder, Eando: CONQUEST OF LIFE

Appendix II

The Best From Startling Stories

Edited by Samuel Mines and published by Henry Holt, New York, in 1953, while he was still editor of Startling Stories, the title of this collection is a misnomer, as only 6 of the 11 stories included are from Startling Stories, the other 5 being from Thrilling Wonder Stories. There is also a foreword and an introduction by Robert A. Heinlein.

Contents

Sturgeon, Theodore: THE WAGES OF SYNERGY (SS, AUG 1953)
McGregor, R. J: THE PERFECT GENTLEMAN (SS, SEP 1952)
Rogers, J. T: MOMENT WITHOUT TIME (TWS, APRIL 1952)
Bradbury, Ray: THE NAMING OF NAMES (TWS, AUG 1949)
Sringer, S: NO LAND OF NOD (TWS, DEC 1952)
Lewis, J: WHO'S CRIBBING? (SS, JAN 1953)
Clarke, Arthur C: THIRTY SECONDS--THIRTY DAYS (TWS, DEC 1949)
Vance, Jack: NOISE (SS, AUG 1952)
Hamilton, Edmond: WHAT'S IT LIKE OUT THERE? (TWS, DEC 1952)
van Vogt, A. E: DORMANT (SS, NOV 1948)
Locke, R. D: DARK NUPTIAL (TWS, FEB 1953)

It was also published by Cassell, London, in 1954 as Startling Stories, and by the Science Fiction Book Club in 1956 as Moment Without Time

Appendix III

The Many Worlds of Magnus Ridolph

Published by Ace paperbacks and in hardcover by Dobson in England, both in 1966, this collection contains four of the Magnus Ridolph stories from Startling Stories, one from Thrilling Wonder Stories, and one from Super-Science Stories.

1. THE KOKOD WARRIORS (TWS)
2. THE UNSPEAKABLE McINCH (SS)
3. THE KING OF THIEVES (SS)
4. THE HOWLING BOUNDERS (SS)
5. SPA OF THE STARS (SS)
6. COUP DE GRACE (Super-Science Stories, 1958)

The Complete Magnus Ridolph

Deluxe hardcover collection published by Underwood-Miller in 1984, for the first time collecting all the Magnus Ridolph stories in one handsome volume.

1. THE KOKOD WARRIORS (TWS)
2. THE UNSPEAKABLE McINCH (SS)
3. THE HOWLING BOUNDERS (SS)
4. THE KING OF THIEVES (SS)
5. THE SPA OF THE STARS (SS)
6. COUP DE GRACE (Super-Science Stories)
7. THE SUB-STANDARD SARDINES (SS)
8. TO BE OR NOT TO C OR TO D (SS) formerly titled COSMIC HOTFOOT
9. HARD LUCK DIGGINGS (SS)
10. SANATORIS SHORT-CUT (SS)